BREAKDOWN

The economic Impact of peak oil

Tim Watkins

Breakdown: The economic impact of peak oil

© Tim Watkins, November 2023.

ISBN: 9798866788408

Contents

Preface

Any attempt to draw the link between energy and the economy immediately runs into the problem of siloed thinking. Mainstream, neoclassical economics simply refuses to consider energy as anything more than a cheap input which may be replaced whenever it suits enough of us to make change politically preferable. To suggest that energy might impose a barrier to economic growth is anathema. As is the suggestion that different energy sources allow for forms of economic activity for which alternative sources could not substitute. Crucially, if one wanted to complete a higher degree in economics and to go on to a lucrative career in banking and finance, it would be in your best interest to keep any ideas you have about the second law of thermodynamics and the likely impact of energy shortages to yourself.

It is for this reason that physicists and oil industry specialists have come to regard economists – along with the politicians they advise – as imbeciles. Indeed, given the economics profession's signal failure to spot every economic crisis in at least the past half century, they have a point. As Michael Gove was to infamously quip during the Brexit campaign (in reference to the 2008 crash):

> "I think the people of this country have had enough of experts *from organisations with acronyms saying that they know what is best and getting it consistently wrong.*"

People forget the last part of that remark. But it speaks to something far more profound than the mere mechanics of a state renegotiating its trading arrangements with a neighbouring trade bloc. Because, as we discovered during the pandemic for example, it turns out the world is jammed full of "organisations with acronyms saying that they know what is best and getting it consistently wrong." And this is a terrifying prospect in a global economy which is as over-complex – and thus extremely fragile – as ours. If we can no longer trust the data produced by the various specialist bodies who gather and publish it, then where else do we turn? If the experts turn out to be self-interested manipulators of information, who else are we to believe? And if the very structure of hierarchical academic silos results in entirely erroneous conclusions about the nature of the world, where else do we turn to find truth?

Prior to the 2008 crash, while lots of us were critical of the self-justifying narratives offered by the various political factions, very few were critical of the information itself. Other than a handful of conspiracy theorists and the deranged academics colonising American social science departments, the majority continued to believe that official agencies, such as the UK's Office for National Statistics or the International Energy Agency, could be relied upon to generate accurate data which we were free to interpret as best we could. After 2008, even this foundation was removed. And we were left playing a game of "triangulation" – taking published data from as wide a range as possible of credible sources, and then trying to tease out the common ground.

One such piece of common ground which I stumbled across while researching what was intended to be a book on the politics of environmentalism in 2015[1], was the complicated set of ideas which came to be known as "peak oil." At its simplest, this was the observation that since oil is a finite resource, there will inevitably come a time when we are producing more than ever before and more than ever again. Not that peak oil is anything like as straightforward as this, because the closer we get to that peak, the more the exporting states are going to curtail exports so as to maintain their own economies. Thus, even before a production peak, oil importing countries may experience shortages. There are thermodynamic issues too – not all oil is equal, and the critical heavy crudes, which are best for producing the diesel, which is the lifeblood of the industrial economy, are declining even before production of all oil has reached a peak. These are all correctives to the simple peak oil story. But while I reference them in this book, my focus here is on what I believe is the first iteration of peak oil – reaching the *economic* peak.

After the 2008 crash, which was preceded by a massive spike in oil prices, economists assumed that we would soon see oil trading at $200-per-barrel or more. This, in turn, would allow oil deposits which had previously been too costly to produce to be drilled. And so, in this way the world would never *run out* of oil. But that isn't what happened. Instead, the collapse in demand across the economy resulted in a steep fall in the need for energy in general and oil in particular. By 2015, the oil price had fallen below $40-per-barrel... far too low for many producers, especially those engaged in hydraulically fracturing the vast shale deposits of the USA. Companies who's offering to investors had been based on permanently higher oil prices suddenly found themselves unprofitable.

In previous periods – notably those during which oil cartels controlled the world oil price – it had been possible to find a Goldilocks price which was low enough for consumers while high enough for the oil companies and their investors. This broke down after 2008, so that we have seen wild swings in the price of oil which benefit neither producers nor consumers. Less obviously but in many ways more importantly, the absence of a stable oil price makes investment across the broad *non-energy* economy far more difficult. This is due to both the direct effect – can a business guarantee that its energy costs won't become unmanageable? – and indirectly – if consumers are forced to spend more on oil products, will they still be able to afford prior levels of consumption?

The answer – to both questions – is no. And this has already had a huge impact on the global banking and financial sector, as banks cease extending credit to anyone – business or household – considered likely to default on their debt. Business development loans and household mortgages are less available, and even governments are having to offer higher interest rates to secure the dollar-denominated lending they need to maintain their activities.

In this book, I will make the case that this growing economic and financial slowdown is the first phase of peak oil playing out in practice. Credit is the point at which the ethereal financial economy and the real – energetic and material – economies meet. And since almost all of the currency in the world is created when banks make loans, as oil gets harder to obtain, a growing "credit crunch" results in bankruptcies and insolvencies as businesses, households and ultimately even governments run out of the (value of the) currency they need to keep going.

Introduction

The two decades 1953 to 1973 saw more trade and economic activity growth than any other period in human history. And yet, beginning around 1970, *something* brought the rate of growth down. The ensuing decade was one of depression as economies failed to recover the vibrancy that they once enjoyed. But then, slowly at first, between 1985 and 2005 we experienced another period of stable growth, albeit at a far lower rate than before. But again, something happened after 2005 to bring growth to a shuddering halt. And, as with the years 1973 to 1983, the period between the Crash and the Covid (2008 to 2020) was one of depression, with anaemic growth at best, bought only by the creation of massive quantities of debt. And even before SARS-CoV-2 embarked on its world tour, the economic indicators were pointing to another downturn – no doubt creating the economic weakness which has underpinned the higher prices, growing debt-defaults and the beginnings of a new economic downturn in the years following lockdown.

Neoclassical economists – who are mostly wrong about everything – find little in common with these periods in our recent past. They talk about "the economy overheating" as a non-explanation for periods of inflation like today and the 1970s. But this is only to give the phenomenon a different name. One, presumably, designed to conjure the image of a pan boiling over when the stove is left on. Insofar as any cause can be found in the mainstream literature, it is the idea of a "wage-price spiral" in which low unemployment empowers workers to demand higher pay which, in turn, causes businesses to raise their prices. Except, of course, that pay had risen faster in the boom years during which unemployment was low despite the demobilisation of thousands of troops following the Second World War.

Even now, economists and central bankers genuflect before the Phillips Curve which wrongly claims a causal link between unemployment and inflation. But today, unemployment has been redefined to the point of farce. In the 1970s, to be unemployed meant not having a full-time, 40-hours-per-week job. Today, someone working for just one hour a week is considered to be employed. And so, despite a massive rate of *under*-employment since 2008, the official rate of unemployment is at an all-time low. Look more closely at data for hours worked and we discover a far weaker economy than the official figures suggest. The same goes for discretionary spending – the amount left over after the bills have been paid. As the establishment media bend over backward to highlight, spending is up. But what they omit is that the figures are only for the amount of money we are collectively spending. Since 2022, the volume of goods and services that we have been buying has fallen. In short, we are buying less but paying more for it.

Nor can economists explain why these inflationary periods come to an end, and what, exactly, ushers in a new round of sustained growth. Most will point to St. Paul Volcker raising the US overnight lending rate to 20 percent in 1980 to explain why inflation was ended. Although even the Fed's own minutes point to the Iranian revolution and the ensuing Iran-Iraq war as the cause of the two recessions between 1980 and 1982 during which inflation came to an end. And it is still far from clear what magic spell brought about the return of sustained growth from the mid-1980s (although some, wrongly, point to the neoliberal policies of Reagan, Mitterrand, and Thatcher).

There is no doubt though that by the 1990s a healthier and less divided economy had emerged from the depression of the early 1980s. this was accompanied by a new political consensus cemented into place by Clinton in the USA and Blair in the UK. Although growth rates never quite returned to the levels between 1953 and 1973, for a large part of the population in the developed states, it appeared as if the good times had returned. Indeed, with the revival of Eastern Europe and Russia following the collapse of the Soviet Union in 1991, and with the incorporation of China into the World Trade Organisation in 2002, the entire world seemed to be on the edge of a new age of prosperity.

Just a few years later though, and it all began to turn sour. Inflation returned to the western economies. And central bankers felt obliged to raise interest rates in an attempt to prevent the inflation becoming embedded. In this, we have to congratulate them. Because not only did the rate rises trigger a wave of debt-defaults which very nearly collapsed the global banking and financial system, but following the 2008 crash, we enjoyed 13 years during which the rate of inflation remained stubbornly below the arbitrary two percent target... so well done them.

Less obviously though, the people nominally in charge of the western economies had presided over – and often accelerated – a geographical fracturing of their national societies. In the UK, this process had been occurring since the end of the First World War, with the old industries in the North of Britain – coal mining, ship building, steel working, etc. – falling into decline even as new industries – automobiles, petrochemicals, aviation, pharmaceuticals, etc. – were bringing new prosperity to the Midlands and the Southeast. A temporary respite occurred during and either side of the Second World War, as governments understood the strategic importance of the older industries in the event that war prevented imports. Moreover, in the aftermath of the war, governments saw unprofitable publicly owned industries as a source of jobs for people (especially demobilised troops) who would otherwise be unemployed.

Even in the 1960s though, the UK government had begun cutting the number of jobs in the nationalised industries. And by the 1970s, with the economy slumping even as inflation was spiralling upward, pressure to cut public spending became unstoppable. Either the nationalised industries would have to stand on their own feet, without public subsidy, or they would be closed down. Some survived – notably British Telecom and British Gas – which formed the backbone of their respective infrastructure networks. Others – like British Steel, British Rail and British Coal – limped on as government hacked away plants, depots and mines, taking large numbers of jobs with them, until just a bare strategic minimum remained.

By 1980, it was commonplace for politicians, economists and journalists to reference a "North-South divide" as a proxy for everything wrong with the economy. But again, this was only to describe the problem in a different way. It provided nothing in the way of an explanation. Which, among other things, is why the early 1980s – and, indeed, the current period – was so divided politically, as the people who self-identify as "left" and "right" (words devoid of much in the way of meaning these days) blamed their opponents for everything wrong with the world.

Nor did the economic malaise end with the division of Great Britain along a line from the Humber to the Severn Estuary. Rather, prosperity continued to retreat away from ex-industrial, rundown seaside and small-town Britain even as a small fraction of the managerial class located in the affluent suburbs around government and finance in London, and adjacent to the top-tier universities, continued to prosper. Indeed, as the new, post-lockdown economy begins to take shape, even those remnants of prosperity have retreated further into a few, tiny, gated and security-guarded enclaves in London and the university towns. At the same time, all talk of "relative poverty" has disappeared, as we witness thousands of households across the UK having to choose between food and heating. Almost every state school across the UK now has to make provision for children arriving unfed and unwashed. And NHS doctors are routinely faced with patients who are malnourished.

Worst of all – at least for social peace – is that the economists, central bankers and politicians never did figure out what caused it. And while they all agree that economic growth would provide the best way out, they have little idea what causes that either. And in the present crisis, that is a visceral problem because if, after promising us that their policies – whether interest rate rises or green new deals – are going to usher in a new age of growth, growth fails to put in an appearance even as most of us continue to experience decline, then we have a recipe for political extremism on a scale that would make Mussolini blush.

So, are these periods of economic stability and instability simply random and inexplicable, or might there be some underlying factor which helps us to explain – at least in broad outline – what was – and is – going on?

Let me begin with the high correlation between energy and per capita GDP across the world's economies (Fig 1). Quite simply, the more access to energy an economy has, the more prosperous its population. Although, of course, the way in which that prosperity is shared varies considerably so that countries with similar access to energy like the UK, USA, Norway and Iceland, have very different levels of income and wealth inequality. Broadly though, the lower a country's access to energy, the lower its per capita GDP.

Now let's examine what has happened to the most important energy source of the past century or so... oil (Fig 2). What we discover – much to the annoyance, by the way, of the advocates of free markets – is that there were three periods of price stability corresponding

Energy use per person vs. GDP per capita, 2021

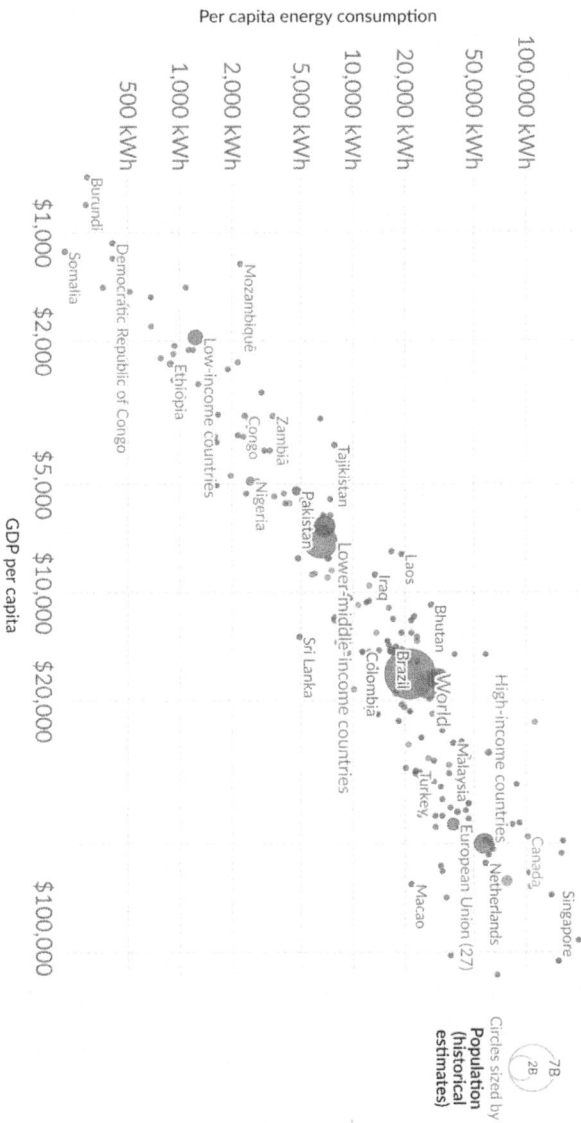

Per capita energy consumption

100,000 kWh
50,000 kWh
20,000 kWh
10,000 kWh
5,000 kWh
2,000 kWh
1,000 kWh
500 kWh

$1,000 $2,000 $5,000 $10,000 $20,000 $100,000

GDP per capita

Burundi
Somalia
Democratic Republic of Congo
Mozambique
Low-income countries
Congo
Zambia
Ethiopia
Nigeria
Tajikistan
Pakistan
Iraq
Laos
Lower-middle-income countries
Colombia
Sri Lanka
Bhutan
Brazil
World
High-income countries
Malaysia
Turkey
European Union (27)
Netherlands
Macao
Canada
Singapore

Circles sized by
Population
(historical
estimates)

7B
2B

Data source: U.S. Energy Information Administration (EIA); Energy Institute Statistical Review of World Energy (2023); Data compiled from multiple sources by World Bank

Note: Energy refers to primary energy – the energy input before the transformation to forms of energy for end-use (such as electricity or petrol for transport).

Figure 1: the link between energy and prosperity

to the rise of cartels – the Rockefeller cartel of the late nineteenth century, the post-war Texas Railroad Commission (TRC) cartel, and the 1970 to 2007 Organisation of Petroleum Exporting Countries (OPEC) cartel. These were then punctuated by periods of boom and bust, corresponding to the periods of economic crisis outlined above.

5

U.S. Crude Oil First Purchase Price

Dollars per Barrel

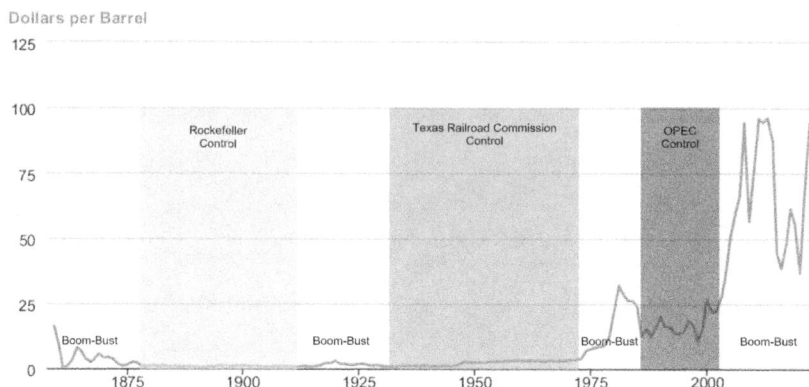

Figure 2: Oil price cartel stability and free-for-all instability

But note that prior to the Second World War, it was coal rather than oil which acted as the world's primary energy source, with only the USA making the transition from coal to oil in the interwar years. As a result, the impact of oil price instability was more muted.

The years when the TRC held prices down were also years when both oil consumption and economic growth grew exponentially. Whereas the period following the TRC's loss of control of oil prices marked the start of the period of stagflation which lasted through the 1970s, with the big jump in oil prices in 1979 as a consequence of the Iranian revolution, ushering in the depression of the early 1980s.

The OPEC cartel was able to impose *some* price stability from the mid-1980s to the early-2000s. But the price of oil remained far higher than under the TRC, corresponding to the period of slower economic growth. And the loss of OPEC control from 2005 fed directly into the crash and ensuing depression from 2008.

Now consider how an oil cartel is able to control prices. It does so by imposing a supply discipline on the various corporations and states involved in the production of oil. If the oil price falls too low, the cartel imposes production cuts which curb supply. In a growing economy, this results in higher prices. In the opposite direction, if prices are too high, the cartel can spur additional production,

6

causing supply to exceed demand and so bring prices down once more.

If oil was infinite, this process could be repeated indefinitely, bringing about a level of economic stability undreamed of in the real world. But oil is not infinite… at least not on any timescale of use to the human economy. Despite the discredited "abiotic oil theory" which holds that oil is produced by chemical reactions within the Earth's core (but which cannot explain why the Earth's surface wasn't awash with oil before humans started burning it in vast quantities) the prevailing consensus is that oil is the result of squillions of plankton-like organisms killed by the deoxygenated shallow seas of the Mesozoic and Cenozoic ages, buried beneath layers of mud, and compressed and heated over millions of years within the Earth's crust – the surviving oil deposits being trapped under pressure in sandstones and shales beneath impermeable cap rocks. In effect, oil like coal, is millions of years' worth of stored solar energy. So that, as chemist turned economist Frederick Soddy was to point out[2], its consumption allowed humans to live beyond our annual solar income for a brief period… "had we but known it, it might have been a merrier age!"

In 1956, a geologist working for Shell – Marion King Hubbert – published a paper[3] which claimed that the oil fields in the continental USA would reach peak production sometime between 1965 and 1970. This was less a prediction than an observation. Based on the average time from discovering a deposit, producing it, and then reaching the point of maximum output, Hubbert reasoned that since peak *discovery* had been in the early 1930s, the peak of production would follow some 35 to 40 years later (Fig 3).

In 1970, some of the US media revisited and mocked Hubbert's prediction because, patently, the USA was producing more oil in 1970 than ever before. As it turned out – at least for conventional oil (i.e., land-based oil under pressure in sandstone held beneath a cap rock which has to be drilled) 1970 also proved to be the high point. For oil deposits beneath the continental USA, Hubbert was right. Peak oil production was reached in 1970.

It was artificial though, at least in part. If the oil beneath the continental USA had been the only oil in the world, you can be sure that the oil companies – supported by western governments – would have done everything they could to keep production rising. And as we discovered after the 2008 crash, there were massive untapped deposits in the source rock and in bitumen sand deposits. But there was no need to do anything so radical in the 1970s and 1980s. Elsewhere in the world, and particularly across the oil crescent which runs north-south from the Caspian Sea in central Asia down to the Persian Gulf and across to North Africa, there were far bigger reserves of conventional oil to be drilled. And since it would be the same oil companies doing the drilling – albeit at the behest of different governments – why worry?

Economically though, the 1970 USA peak – which followed a period of rising costs as the remaining oil became more difficult to extract – marked the point that the TRC lost control of oil prices. Indeed, adjusted for inflation, by 1968, oil prices had returned to their 1950s level. This was nothing compared to the rise from 1970, and especially following OPEC imposing its embargo in October 1973.

The end of the TRC and the rise of OPEC then, correspond to the end of the post-war boom and the beginning of the stagflationary 1970s. There is though, an added dimension to the story... *hubris*. In 1944, economists and central bankers from the allied nations came together in the Bretton Woods resort in New Hampshire to develop a new currency system for the post war years. US negotiators who, like their military counterparts, could never get passed the idea that the British were conning them, rejected Keynes' Bancor proposal – an international currency solely for states to use, and based on the relative imports and exports of each country – which has recently drawn interest because of its similarity to the commodity-backed trading system proposed by the BRICS countries today. Instead, and inevitably given that the US economy was the only one left standing, the conference adopted a hybrid currency system in which the US dollar would be linked to the price of gold (at $35 per ounce) while the rest of the world's currencies would be tied to the dollar.

The most obvious problem with this "Bretton Woods" currency system – which Keynes warned about at the time – was that it created a global dollar shortage which could only be overcome by the USA printing and distributing dollars, initially via the Marshall Aid programme, through which western states could access the dollars they needed to import mostly US goods. In the longer-term, a City of London innovation – the Eurodollar system – would allow

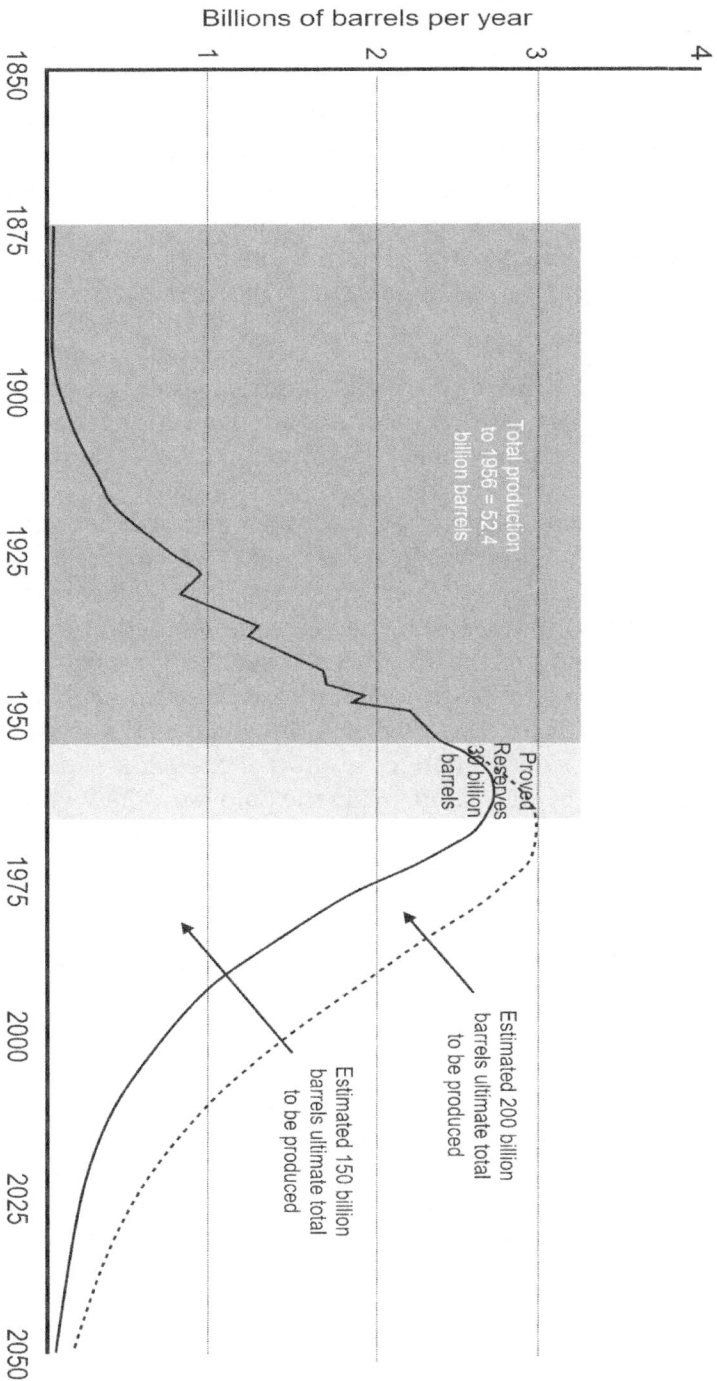

Figure 3: Hubbert's Peak

9

international banks to create dollars out of thin air without any link to or oversight by the Federal Reserve Bank or the US Treasury.

The second problem though, was that US governments might not be able to resist the temptation to print additional dollars as an alternative to properly managing the USA's economy. Sure enough, by the early 1960s, with the Cold War in full swing, a hot war in Indochina warming up, and with governments promising massive social welfare programmes at home, the printing presses started rolling.

So long as the world economy – which, in those days meant mainly North America, Western Europe, Australasia, Japan and South Korea – continued to grow exponentially, the growing influx of dollars in what was becoming a de facto "fiat" currency system seemed to aid the process of economic growth. So that, during the 1953 to 1973 boom, there were few of the financial constraints which had caused recessions in older economies which had used gold to limit currency creation. And again, if oil – and the resource extraction that it enables – had been infinite, the US government might have got away with it. But as the cost of oil production rose and as the oil price increased with it, countries outside the USA which had to trade in dollars began to experience inflation. In effect, the USA had exported the inflation caused by deficit-financing the Cold War, the Vietnam War, the Great Society and the Apollo Moon landings (along with a mountain of graft and pork-barrel politics) to its trade partners. And as those partners – beginning with West Germany – woke up to the fact that they were being asked to pick up the bill, they began to insist that the USA settle accounts in gold – which, if the USA had honoured its $35-per-ounce commitment, ought not to have been a problem.

Briefly, warships traversed the Atlantic taking shipments of gold from the USA to Europe. And in exchange for its gold – but less obvious to the observer – the USA re-imported its inflation. Nixon blamed it on "speculators." But it was really just too much currency chasing too few goods within an economy where rising energy costs had put a brake on further growth. In any case, in August 1971, Nixon called time on the whole thing, and the world has been on a fiat currency system ever since.

Among the reasons why the world didn't return to a gold standard after the Second World War, is that gold standards severely restrict the currency supply, thereby limiting trade and economic growth. Proponents of gold-backed money though, argue that this prevents the monetary excesses enabled by fiat currencies. And they have a point. When the western economies exhausted their potential for exponential growth in the 1970s, further currency creation – which had worked in the 1950s and 1960s – resulted in inflation rather than renewed growth, which ultimately depends upon abundant and cheap energy.

The world climbed out of depression from the mid-1980s in part because the OPEC cartel established a new – albeit higher – stable oil price. This was aided by the opening of new non-OPEC oil fields off Alaska, in the North Sea, and the Gulf of Mexico. This oil too, was more expensive than the oil from the continental USA which had powered the world through the Second World War and the post-war boom. And free from the constraints of a gold-backed currency, the financial corporations in the countries producing this oil were able to use oil receipts to back a massive, debt-based expansion of the currency supply. By the mid-1990s the world was experiencing another boom... although again, not quite as powerful as the one between 1953 and 1973. However, as the saying goes, history doesn't repeat but it often rhymes, and just as the crisis of the 1970s had been about an oil shock undermining a mountain of excess debt. So, in 2005, global conventional oil production peaked, sending oil prices upward. Fearing a return of inflation, the central bankers raised interest rates. And while this did nothing for the price of oil, it served to undermine businesses and households most exposed to interest rates. The term "sub-prime" was to become a household phrase a few years later. But all it really referred to was businesses and households which were vulnerable if the central bankers did anything really dumb... like raising interest rates into a supply shock.

In the run up to the 2008 crash, debt defaults rose, leaving banks holding businesses and houses which they could not sell. And that turned out to be a huge problem because of the mountains of derivatives the banks had created from the predicted income from those business loans and mortgages. Worse still, it turned out that the banks had been using those – now worthless – derivatives as collateral in trading with each other. And so, by raising rates into a deflationary supply shock, the central bankers had succeeded in bringing the western banking system to the edge of collapse.

Collapse was avoided (or perhaps deferred) through quantitative easing – backed by the future taxes of working people across the western economies – and ultra-low interest rates. The unintended consequence of this was what came to be known as "the search for yield." After 2008, investors struggled to find anywhere profitable to put their money. The stock markets held up in large part because it was cheaper for corporations to borrow to buy back their own shares than to offer dividends to investors. As a result, there were fewer companies offering fewer shares, but the share prices kept rising.

This might have served the interest of passive savers. But for investors looking to turn a decent profit, so-called "junk bonds" were the only things offering rates of return similar to pre-2008 returns. And among the best sold junk bonds were those offered by companies engaged in hydraulically fracturing the vast shale deposits of the continental USA. In the financial feeding frenzy which followed, terms like "Saudi America" and the "century of energy independence," became commonplace. Mass media churned out what we might now call "misinformation" about the shale deposits being new discoveries (they had been discovered decades earlier) and fracking as a new technology (it was only its cost which had prevented its earlier use). Investors rushed to throw billions of dollars into companies which could service their debts but never repay them.

It was not entirely the fault of the fracking companies. After 2008, economists had confidently promised that the price of oil would reach $200-per-barrel in the following decade. And if the frackers had been able to sell their oil at that price, things might have been different. But rising oil prices are *deflationary* because the higher cost of primary energy forces businesses and households to shift spending away from the larger, non-energy sectors of the economy in order to meet the higher cost of energy. But as the non-energy sectors shrink, their demand for energy falls accordingly so that, over a period of two to three years – and provided that states don't print new currency – the price of oil falls. Which is exactly what happened as oil from the USA flooded onto the world market. By 2015, and despite OPEC production cuts, the price of oil was back below $40-per barrel. This was enough to allow for a small pick up in general economic growth. But it was disastrous for the fracking companies, many of which went bust even as those remaining struggled to attract new investment.

Briefly, fracking in the USA created a new oil production peak, higher than the peak in 1970. Unlike conventional oil fields – which might continue producing for decades after they are drilled – though, shale well production drops by 90 percent within just three years. Which left the USA locked in a kind of "red queen" situation in which more and more wells had to be drilled just to stand still. And in 2018, depletion overtook new production. In November of that year, global oil production peaked, resulting in higher prices and the beginning of a new recession the following year. This, of course, was overshadowed by the disruption caused by governments as SARS-CoV-2 continued on its world tour.   And although oil production has bounced back from its 2020 low point, it is still some four million barrels a day lower than it had been at the November 2018 peak... and this, despite oil prices settling around $80-per-barrel – which ought to have, but hasn't, encouraged new production.

Meanwhile, with oil prices – and energy and resource prices in general – settling at a new high, the western states stand on the precipice of a new depression. Not least because again, central banks have repeated the mistake of raising rates into a supply shock. At the time of writing, in the UK tens of thousands of households are behind on mortgage and credit card payments. A further 1.4 million mortgage accounts are rolling over in the last quarter of 2023 and the first half of 2024, with an average monthly increase on mortgage payments of around £900... a recipe for a combined debt and housing crisis. Company debt is harder to track – not least because admitting to a problem would likely trigger it – but there may be hundreds of thousands of so-called "zombie companies" which had been managing to service (i.e., pay the interest on) their debts, but with no way of repaying them. As bank lending standards tighten and interest rates rise, this amounts to a ticking time bomb beneath the economy. If we escape with just the "soft landing" promised by the central bankers, we can consider ourselves lucky. But even then, the underlying weakness remains.

My point – and, indeed, the purpose of this book – is to demonstrate the link between the cost of primary energy – oil – and the economy.

And at the core of the argument is the simple observation that, while *useful* energy is finite (barring some yet-to-be-found *energy-dense* and *versatile* alternative to oil) the currency system that we have used throughout the oil age is based on the illusion that energy, and the goods and services it allows us to consume, is infinite. Indeed, for the best part of three centuries of industrial civilisation, this is how it appeared. Detractors like Thomas Malthus – whose warning came before the switch to fossil fuels – were not so much wrong as merely delayed by the once and for good blessing and curse of the industrial use of vast quantities of fossilised sunlight locked up in coal, gas and oil. Today, in contrast, having grown the human population and economy to a high point, there is growing concern that there is no longer enough useful energy to go around. And this, perhaps, is a bigger problem for the so-called "golden billion" – the population of the developed, western states – whose living standards will be impacted hardest by the economic decline which must inevitably follow a final peak in oil production.

Since, like real estate, they don't make oil anymore, the main question to be answered is when peak oil might occur. For some of us, it already has. The UK's all too brief North Sea oil production peaked in 1999 and had fallen by 60 percent by the time the UK became a net importer in 2005. But thus far, solely in terms of volume, world production had held up – at least prior to the ill-advised lockdowns in 2020 and 2021. But as we shall see, there are other dimensions to peak oil which are seldom raised. The energy cost of energy – the amount of energy we need to devote to obtaining energy, and thus the amount that we must divert from the wider economy – imposes a thermodynamic limit[4] prior to any theoretical limit imposed by geology or engineering technology. There may be plenty of fossil fuels in the ground, but if it costs more energy to extract them than they provide in return, they are going to remain in the ground. And then there are questions about the thermal content of new oil deposits – particularly the big shale deposits of the USA and the – currently untapped – shale deposits in Siberia. Instead of high-energy conventional crude, these deposits tend to produce lighter oil, more useful for manufacturing plastic than to powering the heavy transport and machinery that our current way of life depends upon.

This said, the bigger immediate problem is that for decades we have been operating a currency system based on the insane proposition that economic growth – which ultimately means energy and resource growth – can grow exponentially for ever. That is, peak oil – at least until energy shortages become obvious even to an economist – is initially being experienced as a financial crisis and a major economic slowdown. Hence peak oil really is the *economic* predicament of the current period.

Chapter 1

Currency

It may seem odd to begin a discussion of peak oil with an examination of how money is created in the modern world. However, without understanding the process of currency creation – both domestic and international – it is impossible to understand the importance of energy in general, and oil in particular, in the modern economy. Because the way in which our current monetary system operates, effectively rules out sustainability... our economy is like a souffle – it either grows or collapses, but there is no steady state. And since growth requires energy, and most of our energy comes from fossil fuels in general and oil in particular, then oil production *must* grow in line with the currency supply.

Let us begin though, by dispelling a myth. Even today, a majority – including many economists, politicians, and pundits – believe banks operate as building societies or credit unions do. These latter operate as intermediaries between borrowers and depositors, profiting from the spread between the interest rates. But banks operate in a very different way. As the Bank of England explains on its website[5], most of the money in the economy is created when banks make loans:

> "Money is more than banknotes and coins. If you have a bank account, you can use what's in it to buy things, typically with a debit card. Because you can buy things with your bank account, we think of this as money even though it's not cash.

> "Therefore, if you borrow £100 from the bank, and it credits your account with the amount, 'new money' has been created. It didn't exist until it was credited to your account..."

This bank-created currency is known as "bank credit," and can be used either to make payments directly or may be exchanged for cash (for example at an ATM). This type of currency makes up 79 percent of the money in circulation according to the Bank of England. Meanwhile, just three percent comes in the form of notes and coins, with the remaining 18 percent in the form of a special currency called "central bank reserves." This, however, is misleading because these reserves only circulate between banks and the central bank –

they cannot be used to make loans or to pay for goods and services. So that, in terms of currency in circulation among individuals and businesses, bank credit accounts for 96.3 percent, and cash 3.7 percent.

Now let's bust another myth – there is no token. Among those who now understand that currency is created by banks when they make loans, a majority continue to believe that this is done via a "fractional reserve" system which has been in place ever since cheque accounts were invented, and is an extension of the originally corrupt practice of issuing banknotes as a claim on gold or silver (the UK "pound," for example, got its name because it was a claim on a pound – in weight – of sterling silver).

The corruption was that when people first began depositing gold and silver coins in a bank, the bankers would issue a receipt – a "banknote" – in exchange. Most likely, individuals and businesses found it more convenient to swap these banknotes rather than go back and forth to the bank to withdraw and then redeposit the gold and silver. Soon enough, the bankers realised that since depositors only withdrew a tiny fraction of the gold on deposit, they could create many more banknotes than there was gold and silver to back them up... so long, that is, that the economy didn't go bad causing too many people to claim their gold and silver at the same time.

In an age of central banks and cheque accounts, fractional reserve lending came to be institutionalised, with the central bank imposing a "safe" reserve on licenced banks. At a ten percent reserve, banks could generate £1,000 in bank credit for every £100 on deposit. That is, from a deposit of £100, the bank would keep £10 as "vault cash," and then lend the remaining £90. In practice, this meant *depositing* the £90 in the borrower's account. And so, the bank need only keep £9 of the deposit, and could lend out the remaining £81... and so on.

As Nobel Prize-winning chemist turned economist Frederick Soddy[6] was to complain in the wake of the 1929 Wall Street Crash:

> "If the truth were known it would probably be found that this estimate is altogether too modest. At least since, if not before, the War the figures suggest rather a 7 per cent 'safe' limit... On this basis a client depositing £100 of cash in current account

enables the bank to loan £1,330, which at 5 per cent brings in £66 per annum...

"Purely fictitious money, which the nation has not authorised the issue of, is fictitiously lent without anyone giving it up, and then creates perfectly genuine deposits and legal claim upon the community's market for the supply of wealth, indistinguishable in every respect from those the nation has authorised."

This though, was in an age in which the world's currencies were theoretically backed by gold. In the modern economy, currencies are backed only by laws on legal tender, and by states' insistence that individuals and businesses pay their taxes in the national currency. And while central banks maintain the pretence that central bank reserves act as a brake on lending, the true relationship with the banks is the exact reverse. The only constraint on bank lending is the perceived risk of the collateral against which a loan is issued. And as we have witnessed consistently since the 2008 crash, if banks do not have sufficient reserves, the central banks are obliged to issue them.

The same is true within the international "Eurodollar" system. The conceit is that the US Federal Reserve Bank creates all of the dollars which circulate around the world. But again, the truth is the reverse of this. International banks simply create dollar-denominated debt when they make loans to each other, to national governments, and to transnational corporations.

It is, however, the second part of Soddy's complaint which brings us to a central element of the peak oil crisis. This currency, which is spirited out of thin air, and which accounts for almost all of the currency in circulation, is also a "legal claim upon the community's market for the supply of wealth." That is, a claim upon *the future* goods and services created in the economy. And crucially, bank credit comes with interest attached, which means that either the material economy must grow faster than the currency or the value of the currency will be eaten away by monetary inflation (and banks seldom make loans which they believe will be devalued by inflation).

If, hypothetically, we were to gather up all of the currency in existence and immediately pay down all of the outstanding loans, we would find ourselves short. We might be able to pay off the principal, but the interest would remain and, indeed, would compound over time. So that the only way of preventing a crash is for us, collectively, to keep borrowing currency into existence *at a rate* commensurate with the rate of interest minus the rate of inflation.

This though, is where the financial and material economies meet. Because states, businesses, and individuals do not take out loans just to look at the numbers on their bank statements. Rather, we borrow in order to pay for things which we would not otherwise be able to afford. And this is not necessarily a bad thing. A government taking out a loan to fund critical infrastructure, a business borrowing to purchase the latest equipment, or an individual taking out a home improvement loan, may benefit in the long-term, despite having to repay the loan with interest. Banks, on the other hand, must be confident that a government, business, or individual is able to repay the loan before they will agree to it.

As we saw in the fallout from the 2008 crash, banks have developed ways of securitising and insuring the loans they issue, so that the risk is shared with investors. Nevertheless, even with these protections in place, banks need to be confident that their loans – which may be scheduled over 10, 20, or 30 years – will be repaid. In practice, this means that governments have to demonstrate that their national economies – and crucially, the tax taken from them – will continue to grow. In the same way, businesses must provide a credible profit growth forecast, and individuals have to demonstrate that their salaries will continue to grow (welcome to the greasy pole).

Problems begin when banks – domestic and international – decide that the risk of default is too high. This could be a hard default in which borrowers simply lack the currency to repay or even service their debts, or it might be a soft default in which inflation erodes the real value of the repayments. Either way, in such circumstances – as happened prior to 2008 and is happening again in 2023 – banks tighten their lending standards and increase the interest rates on their loans. So that, across the economy, the amount of currency in circulation falls, causing a recession or a crash.

The bottom line is that banks only make loans if they are confident that the economy will continue to grow, and that a slowdown or fall in the rate of growth will cause banks to pull currency out of the system. But the only way the economy can continue to grow is if our exploitation of the material world grows accordingly. And since oil remains at the heart of our energy and material mix, we simply have to maintain the rate at which oil production grows.

Chapter 2
The Energy Theory of Value

Adam Smith gave us a fairy tale about barter. So powerful is this myth, that I will wager that if you stop someone in the street and ask them why money was invented, they will answer that it was to make the process of bartering easier. Barter, however, only occurs on a large scale in post-industrial economies which have collapsed. Barter was widespread, for example, in post-soviet Russia, in Zimbabwe in the 1990s, and on Puerto Rico after the 2017 hurricane. It was not though, common in the English villages of the Middle Ages.

Indeed, the system of exchange among peasants was about as close as anyone has come to Karl Marx's "from each according to his abilities to each according to his needs" – although with a large element of the Mafia thrown in. That is, the English village operated on favours, which bound people into an ongoing relationship with each other. If I needed eggs, you were bound to provide them. But this meant that I owed you a favour... and woe betides me if I failed to honour the obligation. Not that these transactions went entirely unrecorded. The Bank of England, for example, has a large collection of tally sticks – notches would be cut into the stick to indicate a debt, and then the stick would be split lengthways so that each party could keep a record. Other cultures have used knotted strings, shells, and stones to record obligations. But consideration of precise value was primarily the concern of the wealthy, travelling merchants, and the military.

Indeed, funding the military is likely the reason money was created in the first place. In all non-agrarian societies, dwellings tend to be the same size. But once people settled into agrarian economies, one building was always bigger than the others... the granary. Not long after, the dwelling adjacent to the granary also grew in size. Until, eventually, the first palaces were created. And next to both granary and palace was another large building... the barracks.

The first money was likely invented to support the occupants of the barracks – soldiers whose job was not just to protect the grain, but also to travel the kingdom collecting that part of the annual harvest to be paid as a tax. Unlike the peasants living off the land, the soldiers had no ongoing relationship with the people. And so, a favour-based system of exchange wouldn't work. This might leave the travelling soldiers unable to trade for a bed and a meal – they might take these by force, but only at the cost of civil unrest. If, however, the soldiers could be paid with money – which the villagers would be required to use to pay their taxes – then the soldiers could pay for a bed and a meal without upsetting the villagers.

Systems of obligation broke down with the coming of industrialisation and the movement of people from the land into the cities. The anonymity of urban environments made it all too easy to cheat and to avoid the old informal sanctions used against cheats. Furthermore, the development of company stores allowed the early capitalists to operate a money system which mirrored the national tax system – workers could be paid with tokens which could only be redeemed in the company store. But even where this practice did not operate, urban living created a demand for some means of exchange which reflected the end of the ongoing village relationships. And since no obligation was expected, the need to determine value began to exercise the thinkers of the day.

In his *Wealth of Nations*, Adam Smith made the case that socially necessary labour time determines value:

> "If among a nation of hunters, for example, it usually costs twice the labour to kill a beaver which it does to kill a deer, one beaver should naturally exchange for, or be worth two deer. It is natural that what is usually the produce of two days' or two hours' labour, should be worth double of what is usually the produce of one day's or one hour's labour."

One philosopher who sought to develop this "labour theory of value" (while failing to take note of the growing use of steam power) was a young German who had moved to England from his hometown of Trier in the Rhineland. The young Karl Marx embraced Smith's labour theory of value but was puzzled about its application to profit. The difficulty was that, if all of the inputs to industry were exchanged for what they were worth, then it would be impossible for capitalists to make a profit. Logically, one or more inputs to the process had to be paid less than it was worth... and somehow the capitalists had to be appropriating the difference.

Marx's solution – which has just enough truth to it to give credence to the theory as a whole – was "the money trick." By paying money in exchange for the workers' *time*, the capitalists obscure the value of the labour the workers actually perform. In this way, Marx argued, profit was the surplus labour of the working class. No doubt even some of the inequality in modern economies stems from the ability of employers to act in this way. And at the time Marx was formulating these ideas, British industry remained very labour-intensive.

Coal-powered industrialisation, however, put labour in its correct place. The explosion in production which followed the development of the steam engine to the point that it transported thousands of tons of goods on the new railways, and millions of tons across the oceans on the new steamships could not have occurred using labour power alone. So that, toward the end of his life, even Marx began to question if all of that machinery might also be a source of value.

Marx was wrong about that too. The machines, like labour, were merely the means by which value is harnessed in an economy. But he had been entirely correct to surmise that some input to the productive process *must* be being paid less than it was worth. But the *real* money trick involves paying by the hour for work on a geological timescale.

Neither Marx nor Smith would have known that the coal used to drive the machines was fossilised plants laid down and compressed over hundreds of millions of years. As Soddy put it a century later:

> "All the requirements of pre-scientific men were met out of the solar energy of their own times. The food they ate, the clothes they wore, and the wood they burnt could be envisaged, as regards the energy content which gives them use-value, as stores of sunlight. But in burning coal one releases a store of sunshine that reached the earth millions of years ago...

> "The flamboyant era through which we have been passing is due not to our own merits, but to our having inherited accumulations of solar energy from the carboniferous era, so that life for once has been able to live beyond its income. Had it but known it, it might have been a merrier age!"

But nobody has ever paid for the work provided by those millions of years of fossilised sunlight, only for the work required to dig the stuff out of the ground... which had been particularly easy in Great Britain, where coal seams jutted out of the side of the hills. A ton of coal contains roughly the equivalent of a year of work (based on an eight-hour-day) a heavy horse provides, or five-and-a-half years of human labour. But not one of the mining companies which were essential to the industrial revolution would have paid even the tiniest fraction of this to the miners for each ton they dug out of the ground... had they have done so, they would have been bankrupt within a week! According to Guy Samuel Solomon[7], a Tyneside miner in the 1830s might have been paid as little as three shillings and sixpence (£11.80 adjusted for inflation) per ton of coal – less than the hourly minimum wage today, and far less than the £183,711 price of 5.5 years of human labour at today's average wage.

In the modern economy, oil – which is more energy-dense than coal – provides an even greater return. A tonne of oil provides a full eleven years' worth of human labour. Which works out at roughly 4.5 years per barrel. That's the equivalent of £150,309 worth of work for the $85 or so that a barrel currently trades at – that's a 2,000:1 return on investment... which is precisely why oil-powered industrial capitalism has generated such huge profits for the owning classes while simultaneously – at least until recently – raising the living standards of people in the developed and developing states.

Labour is, of course, a very weak source of energy. And insofar as value is an entirely human concept, then we must not underestimate the role of human ingenuity in the creation of value. Nevertheless, in the modern world it is inanimate energy in general, and oil in particular, which is the source of almost all of the value generated in the economy.

We should, however, acknowledge the criticism made by many detractors of the labour theory of value, that in fact, there is no source of value beyond the price that someone is prepared to pay for a good or service at any time. This is persuasive insofar as the financial economy is a poor reflection of the material economy it is based on. The price of a car or a fridge or a washing machine is more likely to reflect the subjective assessments of buyers (how much they are prepared to pay) and sellers (how high they can set the price) rather than some objective external source of value. But this only works in the short-term – if the price people were prepared or able to pay for those items fell below the cost of manufacturing and distributing them (including the interest on loans and dividends to investors) for any length of time, the companies involved would simply shut up shop.

This is why the material economy matters. And since energy is the source of value – the driving force behind the material economy – it is why we ought – although conventional economists do not – place energy at the heart of our understanding of the economy.

Chapter 3

Energy and Complexity

Perhaps the most enduring myth of our age is the one which sees history as an upward arc of progress. It is superficially seductive. Certainly, we live in an age of unprecedented scientific and technological miracles. Where the Gods of Olympus limited themselves to jaunting around the islands of the Aegean Sea, we think nothing of boarding kerosene-powered aluminium tubes to fly from one end of the Earth to the other at speeds in excess of 500mph, while entertaining ourselves with smartphones connected to a global internet via a network of geostationary satellites surrounding the planet.

Almost all of the technology that we take for granted would seem like magic to a fourteenth century European peasant, or even to a nineteenth century factory worker. This though, is where the paint begins to flake off the "ever upward arc of progress" myth, because almost all of our technology would be easily understood by an American factory worker in the 1950s. As physicist Tom Murphy[8] explains:

> "Look around your environment and imagine your life as seen through the eyes of a mid-century dweller. What's new? Most things our eyes land on will be pretty well understood. The big differences are cell phones (which they will understand to be a sort of telephone, albeit with no cord and capable of sending telegram-like communications, but still figuring that it works via radio waves rather than magic), computers (which they will see as interactive televisions), and GPS navigation (okay: that one's thought to be magic even by today's folk). They will no doubt be impressed with miniaturization as an evolutionary spectacle, but will tend to have a context for the functional capabilities of our gizmos.

> "Telling ourselves that the pace of technological transformation is ever-increasing is just a fun story we like to believe is true. For many of us, I suspect, our whole world order is built on this premise."

In any case, while the progress myth *appears* to work through the evolution of the industrial economy, on a longer timeframe, the myth breaks down. Indeed, less historically aware visitors to British museums often wonder whether the exhibits are in the wrong order when they see the primitive (and sustainable) Anglo-Saxon economy taking up the five centuries *after* the multinational Roman economy. The period after the Black Death and the European 30-years war (and the associated civil war in England) mark similar, if less enduring, descents into dark ages.

The latter two examples of economic and social reversal are related to "little ice ages," which resulted in poor harvests, greater malnutrition and susceptibility to disease. Insofar as these pre-industrial economies ran entirely on renewable energy and were thus at the mercy of the amount of solar energy converted into calories by food crops, we might argue that decline was a consequence of a loss of primary energy. The same – in a different manner – goes for the Western Roman Empire which, among its many political failings, over-consumed the trees which were the source of wood and charcoal for building and energy. Indeed, the stark difference between the plentiful Roman ruins and the sparce archaeology left by their Ango-Saxon successors is explained by the latter settling for a much lower energy-based economy which, among other things, rendered stone building too energy-expensive to be worth the effort.

Stone building returned with the Normans, as evidenced by the many ruined castles dotted around western Europe. But it was only really in the eighteenth century that European architecture overtook the Romans. And by that time, the origins of industrialisation were in place.

Historians still argue about why industrialisation only happened when it did. After all, the coal which powered the British Empire to world hegemony in the nineteenth century had been available to the Romans had they chosen to use it. But for all their ingenuity, the Romans left the coal in place, and limited their iron and steel making to primitive kilns and manual smithies. The mere presence of coal, iron ore and limestone, then, was not sufficient to trigger an industrial revolution.

A more plausible explanation revolves around trade. Immediately prior to the industrial revolution, the western Europeans had settled colonies around the Atlantic and Caribbean. And trade between these colonies provided goods – such as cotton – in quantities great enough to make industrial production worthwhile. At the same time, the expansion of trade created the capital which could be invested in new machinery and factories. Less obviously though, the Atlantic trade provided several substances which were to drive the intellectual revolution which provided the scientific and technological framework for the industrial revolution.

As with industrialisation, we have to ask why an Enlightenment didn't happen much earlier. After all, the classical philosophy on which the Enlightenment was built was available to the Romans, the Normans, the Habsburgs and the Tudors. Indeed, the early Romans also had access to the Great Library of Alexandria, which contained sources unknown even to eighteenth century Europe. Again, it was energy along with the Atlantic trade which provided the basis for a European Enlightenment.

Another of our failings is our inability to understand the psychological, social, political and economic circumstances of people from different historical periods. And among the differences, understanding the impact of malnutrition and disease in earlier periods is one of the more difficult. In an economy which, even in the hands of profiteering companies, delivers clean drinking water from a tap and a mass of food in a nearby supermarket, it is hard to put yourself in the place of someone whose lack of calories clouds his thinking and who spends his days in a mild alcoholic haze from drinking small beer as the healthiest alternative to the bacteria-infested pond or stream water in most towns and villages. The arrival of alternative drinks from the Americas had a dramatic impact. As Stephen Hicks[9] explains:

> "The impact of the introduction of coffee into Europe during the seventeenth century was particularly noticeable since the most common beverages of the time, even at breakfast, were weak 'small beer' and wine… Those who drank coffee instead of alcohol began the day alert and stimulated, rather than relaxed and mildly inebriated, and the quality and quantity of their work improved… Western Europe began to emerge from an alcoholic haze that had lasted for centuries."

Nor was it solely the use of a drink that required boiled – and thus safer – water that fed into the Enlightenment. As Angela Jansz and Tracey Taylor[10] explain:

"Prior to Spanish exploration of the Americas, Europe of the old world had a very limited repertoire of psychoactive substances. There was no opium, caffeine (in the form of tea or coffee), no tobacco or cannabis and the native European solenaceous hallucinogens and other herbs used in healing were enmeshed in superstition or dispensed with limited understanding by apothecaries.

"There really was only one psychoactive drug, alcohol. It had to fulfil a wide range of social, medicinal and intoxicating functions."

The products arriving in Western Europe from the Atlantic trade in previously undreamed-of quantities served both to awaken and alter the minds and thoughts of those consuming them. But while necessary to the Enlightenment, these would have been as nothing if the population had remained so malnourished that they lacked the energy to do more than fall into bed after a day's work. Energy, in the form of dense and easily available calories was also necessary. And this was obtained from imported root vegetables along with a substance which has been referred to as "pure, white and deadly[11]."

Today we think of sugar as something of a toxin – so common in processed foods that it has generated an epidemic of metabolic diseases. But in calorie-starved medieval Europe, sugar was a prized luxury. And the Atlantic trade ushered in a massive increase in its consumption. As Jonathan Hersh and Hans-Joachim Voth[12] explain:

"While medieval Cyprus produced no more than an estimated 50-100 tons of sugar per year, Santo Domingo in the 18th century alone produced 3,500 tons. England in 1700 imported approximately 10,000 tons; a century later, this figure had risen to 150,000 tons, according to some estimates.

"As the price of sugar declined, consumption spread to the lower classes. It was frequently used as a substitute for a protein source, consumed in the absence of meat when and where meat was too expensive. Though the simple carbohydrates from sugar do not have all the nutritional qualities of a protein source, its consumption offered calories at a time where energy availability may have severely constrained labor input. In addition, sugar was used to add sweetness and calories to food and drink, especially to tea or coffee, or added in liquid or powdered form to a whole range of foods."

In these four strands – the increased wealth from trade, the development of a safe and stimulating drink, the additional consumption of a range of stimulants including tobacco and cocaine, and the massive energy boost from sugar, we have the basis for an Enlightenment. And it is no accident that it began in the Salons of Paris and the Coffee Houses of London.

While most people associate the industrial revolution that followed with coal and steam-power, historian Eric Hobsbawm includes in his book, *Industry and Empire* the line[13], "he who says industry says cotton." This is because the first industrial machinery radically overhauled the way in which cloth was produced. And again, the driver for the change was the Atlantic trade. Cotton – picked using the labour of African slaves – was arriving in Britain in quantities far greater than was needed for domestic production. And so, in the eighteenth century, the industrial cotton mills of Lancashire began the production of cotton cloth for export. Why Lancashire? Because of the high, steep sided valleys which provided abundant – although intermittent – waterpower.

Not that cotton production was the only process to make use of waterpower. For centuries, mill races had been excavated to allow water wheels to power flour mills and blacksmith bellows. Water wheels reinforced with iron could handle and transfer more energy than the older, wooden wheels. And with the growth in production for export, the demand for bigger and more robust water wheels fed into the growth of that other mainstay of the industrial economy… iron working.

Iron working at the scale required by export manufacturing, in turn, required the switch from charcoal to hotter and more abundant coal to power the furnaces. And it is no accident that the first industrial iron works turned up in British river valleys – like the Severn Gorge – where water, iron ore and coal was easily available in massive quantities.

It is only after the early, and easy, coal deposits were depleted that the use of steam power became widespread. The first Newcomen beam engines developed by Thomas Newcomen in 1712, made use of a small quantity of the coal recovered from deeper mines to pump out water which would otherwise have flooded the mines. By 1730, these atmospheric steam engines were common across the mining districts of Britain. But they were inefficient – most of the potential energy from the coal simply vented as waste heat into the atmosphere.

We then saw a process which is common to all energy technologies – something that economists, even though they don't understand it, refer to as "productivity gains." At its simplest, productivity means doing more for less. What this actually means is to use technology – in the broadest sense of the word – to convert more of the potential energy into work, and to create less waste heat as a by-product. In the 1770s just up the road from where Adam Smith was making up misinformation about the economy – James Watt, an engineer at Glasgow University developed a more efficient steam engine which incorporated a separate condensing chamber to capture and harness a large part of the previously wasted heat, providing power on both the upward and downward stroke of the engine.

It was this far more powerful steam engine which provided the basis of the revolution in transport which began during the Napoleonic Wars, and which saw Britain emerge as the first truly industrial nation from the 1820s. And again, we find the process of productivity gain across those technologies too. There were huge advances, for example, in railways between Trevithick's 1804 journey down the Taff Valley from Merthyr to Abercynon (the empty train having to be towed back up the valley with horses) and the opening of the Liverpool to Manchester railway in 1830. In a similar way, productivity advances allowed steam ships to advance from the early and inefficient paddle steamers to the oceangoing giants of the late nineteenth and early twentieth centuries.

But rather like energy sources themselves, technologies go through a "low-hanging fruit" process in which we move from the cheap and easy to the difficult and expensive. In 1938, Gresley's Pacific class locomotive *mallard* set the steam railway world record of 126mph. Although more than a century and a plethora of productivity improvements between them, the core technology was the same as

Trevithick's 1804 engine and Stephenson's *Rocket* quarter of a century after that. But while Stephenson had made use of a raft of cheap and easy improvements, such as improved sleepers and bevelled wheels, Gresley had had to push the limits of steam engineering to squeeze the last few miles per hour out of *Mallard*. And, indeed, the cost of the Pacific class locomotives was far too high for the economy of the 1930s to bear – contributing to the bankruptcy of Britain's railway companies and resulting in de facto nationalisation during the Second World War.

Another way of viewing this process of technological and energetic response to changes in production and trade is to think about it as a process of adding – and responding to – *complexity*. To be clear, this is not the same as "complicated," but rather refers to a system developing a growing number of *discrete* moving parts whose combination determines the nature of the system as a whole.

Had you been able to use a time machine to travel back to Western Europe in the year 1490, you would have found yourself in an impoverished and apparently irrelevant backwater of the Eurasian continent. The received wisdom of the age was that the future belonged to one or both of the major powers of the age – the Ottomans in the Middle East and the Ming Empire in the Far East. The idea that the constantly warring nations on the European peninsula might rapidly develop empires of their own, and that three of these – the Spanish, French, and British – might between them dominate most of the world's habitable landmass would have been laughable. And yet, through a process of adding and responding to complexity, this is precisely what happened.

To return to the textiles which lay at the heart of industrialisation. In the fifteenth and sixteenth centuries, luxury items like silk and lace were available as imports for the very wealthy. But almost all of the cloth used by ordinary people was a product of domestic labour by women, who were able to combine spinning and weaving cloth with childrearing. Indeed, prior to the Atlantic trade and the growing abundance of cotton, most of the cloth was from wool. The growing availability of cotton, and the superiority of cotton over wool, created the basis for a shift in textile manufacture from the home to the manufactory – the invention of early industrial machines, like Hargreaves' spinning jenny and Arkwright's water powered weaving frame, providing the means to produce in large quantities.

Rather than looking at a process – whether mining, weaving or railways – it is often what is occurring outside which highlights the complexity. Once weaving requires more than human labour, for example, a waterwheel and gearing industry is required to allow the harnessing of cascading water. And, as we have seen, once the need for energy outstrips the capacity of wooden wheels and gears, a new iron – and later steel – industry is required to brace the wheels and to prevent the gears from stripping. Once such an iron and steel industry has been developed, its product can then rapidly advance other sectors of the economy, for example, the use of steel ploughshares helping to boost agricultural yields. But to have an iron industry, we need coal, which, as mines get deeper, require steam engines which, in turn, provide the basis for locomotives and railways. Soon enough, the horse drawn canal barges are overtaken by railways connecting the coal and the iron, and the finished products to the end users. And by the early nineteenth century, the textile mills were doing away with waterpower in favour of more powerful and reliable steam engines.

Often hidden from history, one of the ways in which colonisation worked (and makes it different to imperialism) is via a ban on the manufacture of goods in the colonies. While, for example, the American revolution is remembered as a revolt against the hubristic attempt by Britain's aristocracy to levy taxes on the American colonists to pay for the earlier war with France, the simmering discontent came from the insistence that the colonists buy manufactured goods and textiles from Britain. After the American colonies gained independence, the British decimated Indian cotton manufacture – including in the home – so as to force Indians to import British cloth. In this way, the Atlantic trade – and later world trade – served to bring vast wealth back to the capitalist class in Britain, allowing for further investment in industrialisation which created even more complexity.

Imperialism, which is often treated as the same thing as colonialisation, added an entirely new level of complexity via a growing global banking and financial system. Rather than crudely forcing the import of goods from the mother country, imperialism worked by indebting the subject country. Argentina, for example, while never formally colonised, has never survived the imposition of usuary-like interest rates levied on the loans provided to build its infrastructure – infrastructure, ironically, which benefited Britain more than its indigenous farmers, whose beef became a staple of the British diet. Something similar was done to the Ottoman colony of Egypt, when the British and French provided the finance, materials and skilled engineers to build the Suez Canal (which, again, benefitted the British more than the Egyptian people). When Egypt's rulers struggled to repay the loan, the British simply turned up and declared Egypt a "Protectorate," despite it still officially remaining within the Ottoman Empire.

Even less obvious in this process of adding complexity is the role of *surplus* energy. That is, the energy left over for economic use after the energy to generate energy has been consumed. We saw a hint of this with the first Newcomen beam engines used to pump water from coal mines. A small quantity of coal from the mine had to be set aside to power the beam engine, with only the remaining coal being available to the wider economy. As railway and steamship transportation grew, greater proportions of coal had to be diverted into supplying energy, leaving a smaller proportion to the wider economy – although, because the overall volume of coal being produced was expanding even faster, this relative shift in the proportion of surplus energy did not hinder the growth of the industrial economy as a whole.

A similar process was occurring with human and animal power. Humans are powered by the hydrocarbons in food, which we have evolved to convert into muscle and brain power. But whereas in the fifteenth and sixteenth centuries most people were engaged in food production, by the end of the nineteenth century, this had fallen to around a quarter of us, and today it is less than two percent. In part, the import of foods via the Atlantic trade allowed more workers to move (often against their will) from agriculture to industry. In part, industry itself provided means – like traction engines – to dispense with human and animal labour. Thus, food production and consumption became increasingly complex.

Complexity itself, then, is a product both of the search for and the harnessing of ever more surplus energy. But it is also subject to limits. The Atlantic trade was about as advanced as it is possible to be using renewable energy alone. A better understanding of ocean currents, trade winds and tides allowed Europeans to utilise the most efficient trade routes, while bigger and sturdier ships provided the means to plant and supply colonies across the American continents. But without the harnessing of far more energy-dense coal, that was as good as it was going to get. And as American (and less well-known Haitian) independence demonstrated, maintaining control of trade using renewable energy was impossible in the face of determined resistance.

Coal power provided the first reliable(ish) shipping timetables and allowed for more direct ocean crossings. Moreover, coal powered iron and steel ships could transport vastly more goods (and later passengers) than was possible with wooden sailing ships. In a sense then, coal made the world both bigger (economic growth) and smaller (transport times) than it had been. It also allowed Britain's Royal Navy – bigger than its two biggest rivals combined – to exercise control over world trade, via a network of coaling stations, in a way that a sail-powered navy never could. But even as the Royal Navy reached the peak of its power in the decade prior to the Great War, two processes combined to signal its decline.

In 1911, the crisis in Morocco prompted the European powers to send warships. To the horror of the British Admiralty, one of the new German gunboats sailing from Wilhelmshaven more than 100 miles to the east, arrived off the coast of Morocco before the British. The German ship, it turned out, had the advantage of using a better fuel than coal... oil. Not that oil-based technology had caught up. The ship still burned fuel in a bunker to boil water into steam. It was just that kilogram for kilogram, the oil – which was easier to load and store – provided more heat than coal... and that translated into greater speed. Two years later, British coal production peaked. And unlike the USA, whose economy had already overtaken Britain and Germany, Britain had little access to oil.

Although it would take another half century for the European economies to complete the transition from coal to oil power, and to develop the new technologies to harness this new energy source, the foundation of an even more complex oil age had been laid. And even without the ruinous wars between 1914 and 1945, the USA was already best placed to emerge as the winner of the oil age.

Chapter 4

Oil in the modern economy (1: Energy)

For most of us, oil is synonymous with energy, although, ironically, oil is seldom used directly to power anything. Sure, some oil deposits are light enough that they are equivalent to the bunker fuels which power some ships. This, for example, is why from 1943 to 1945, the Japanese Navy was based in Sumatra, where local oil could be used without the need to refine it. In most cases though, oil must go through a complex and expensive refining process to separate out the various fuels which we use day-in, day-out across the economy.

Although the density and energy content of crude oil varies from deposit to deposit, an average barrel of oil (42 US gallons) provides us with:

- 42.7% Petrol (gasoline)
- 27.4% Diesel
- 5.8% Aviation fuel
- 5% Heavy (e.g., ship) fuel
- 4% Asphalt
- 3% Light (e.g., home boiler) fuel
- 2% condensates (e.g., lighter fuel)
- 10.1% Petrochemical feedstock and residual fuels.

These amounts vary across the world, because there are more than 70 grades of crude oil, accounting for viscosity and sulphur content, and because each refinery is calibrated to produce different volumes of the various oil products. Another way of breaking down oil products is by looking at the sectors of the economy where they are consumed. In 2019, global oil consumption rose above 100 million barrels of oil per day, although since the pandemic, consumption has failed to return to that level. The refined products for those 100m or so barrels a day fuel economic growth across the economy. In 2020, the share of those 100m barrels across the OECD economies[14] was:

- 48.6 Road transport
- 16.2 Petrochemicals
- 9.8 Agriculture, residential and commercial

- 4.4 Aviation
- 3.6 Marine fuel
- 3.0 Electricity generation
- 1.8 Rail and inland waterways
- 12.6 Other industry.

The chart below (Fig 4) shows how petroleum products flow through the UK economy. Obviously, different countries use petroleum differently according to how their economies are configured. The UK has a relatively small industrial base and is highly dependent upon imports, and so most of its oil consumption is in transport. China, in contrast, is an industrial powerhouse, and so its oil consumption is more evenly spread across industry, agriculture, and construction (Fig 5).

This provides an important corrective to the claims made by politicians and journalists in western states like the UK, that we have gone a long way to "de-carbonising" our economies and have made big reductions to our oil consumption. While this *appears to be true* on the face of it – UK oil consumption has declined steadily since its high point in 1973 – one reason for this is that governments since 1980 chose to offshore British manufacturing to other parts of the world, where they could take advantage of cheap labour and fewer regulations (Fig 6).

The result – because the western states have continued to grow consumption – is that global oil consumption has grown remorselessly, despite growing alarm over the impact this is having on the environment, irrespective of decades of treaties and domestic policy reforms, and despite claims that "we are all doing our bit" to reduce our carbon footprints. This is not just a matter of hypocrisy or western duplicity. The fact of the matter is that, at our current level of science and engineering, we have no energy source to come near to replacing the benefit we derive from oil. Certainly, around the edges we can make a difference. Battery electric vehicles, for example, can reduce demand for petrol – although in China's case, they have been developed to use coal *indirectly* rather than the precious oil required by their export economy. But petrol is not really the issue. Indeed, I would argue that in economic terms, petrol is close to a waste product.

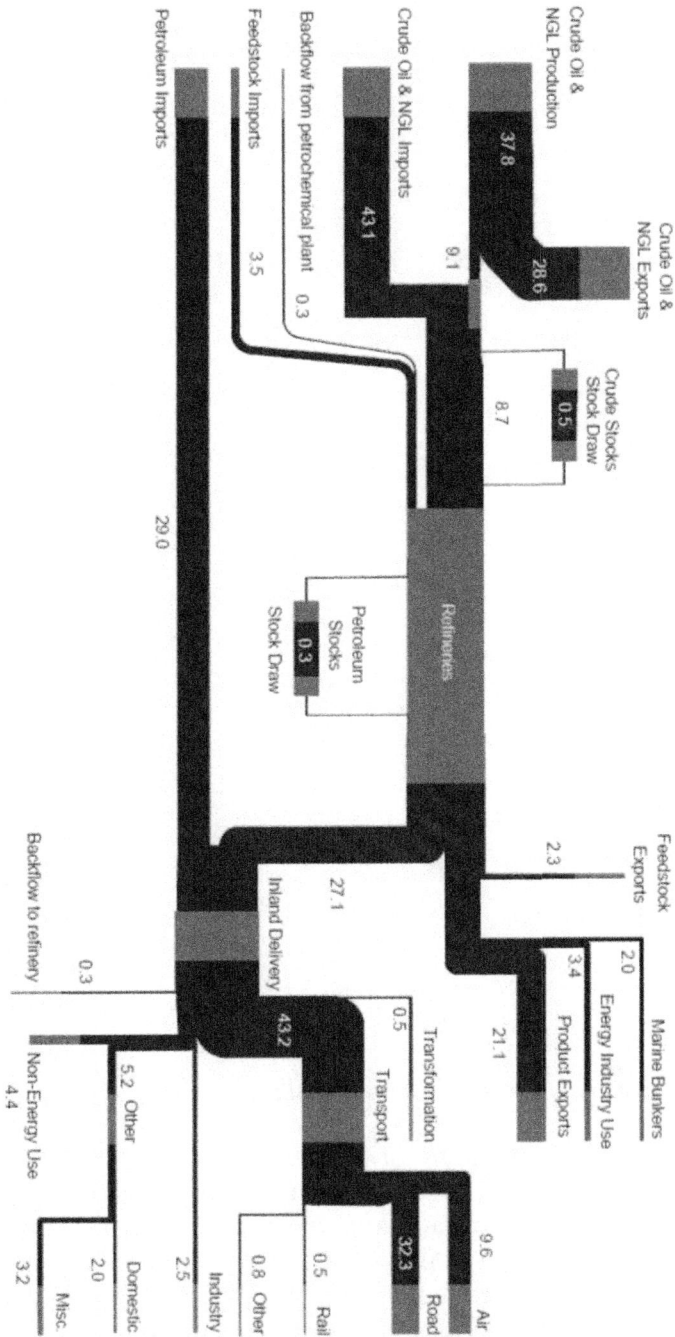

Petroleum flow chart 2022 (million tonnes)

Crude Oil & NGL Production
Crude Oil & NGL Imports
Backflow from petrochemical plant
Feedstock Imports
Petroleum Imports

37.8
43.1
9.1
28.6
0.3
3.5

Crude Oil & NGL Exports

Crude Stocks Stock Draw   0.5
8.7

Petroleum Stocks Stock Draw   0.3

Refineries

29.0

Feedstock Exports   2.3

Inland Delivery

Backflow to refinery   0.3

27.1

Non-Energy Use
4.4

5.2 Other

Marine Bunkers   2.0
Energy Industry Use   3.4
Product Exports   21.1

43.2

Transformation   0.5

Transport

32.3

9.6   Air
0.5   Road
0.8   Other
Rail
Industry   2.5
Domestic   2.0
Misc.   3.2

Figure 4: UK oil flow

Source: Department for Energy Security and Net Zero - Digest of UK Energy Statistics 2022.

Refined oil

Loss during processing and transportation

Loss: 2,385.1

Other petroleum products: 30,591.2

Other petroleum products

Fuel oil: 3,138.5

Fuel oil

Diesel: 24,482.8

Diesel

Kerosene: 4,694.1

Kerosene

Gasoline: 18,267.6

Gasoline

Note: Other petroleum products include lubricating oil, paraffin, solvent oil, petroleum coke, refinery dry gas and others. Because of limited data and resources, the import and export of various oil products are not considered in this flowchart.

Others · Residential · Wholesale parts · Transportation · Construction · Agriculture · Industrial raw materials · Industry

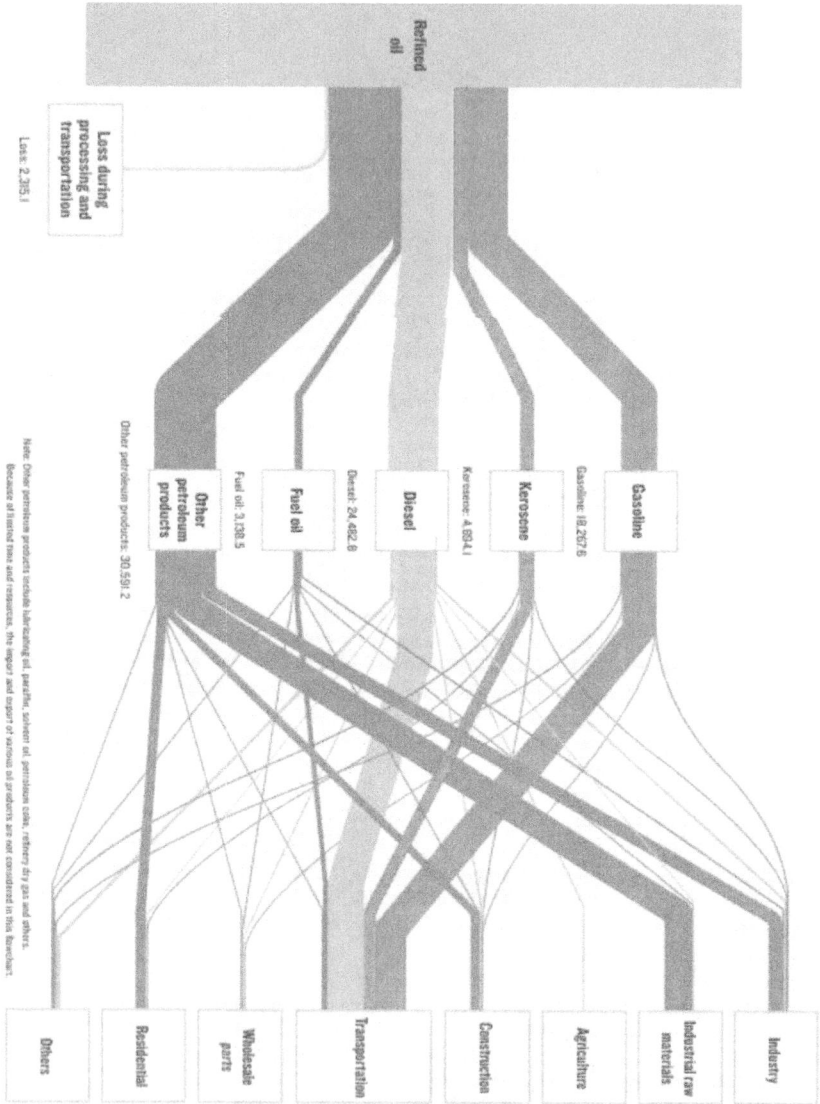

Figure 5: China oil flow

Diesel is the real lifeblood of the economy. At our current technological level, diesel is the only fuel that can run our heavy agricultural, industrial, mining and construction machinery. It is also the only fuel which can power large trucks and trains over the long distances that our economies depend upon. And again, while there has been some tinkering around the edges – for example, trams, buses and refuse collection trucks can run on electricity

42

Oil consumption

Oil consumption is measured in terawatt-hours (TWh).

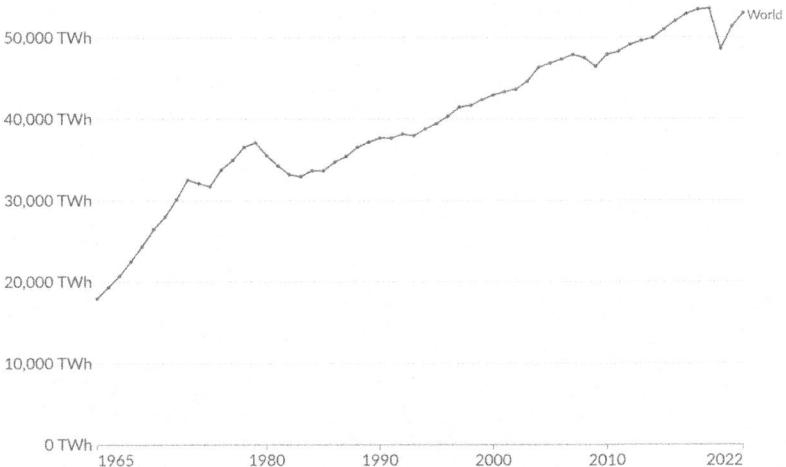

Source: Energy Institute Statistical Review of World Energy (2023)

OurWorldInData.org/fossil-fuels • CC BY

Figure 6: UK v World oil consumption

(taking advantage of regenerative braking) or hydrogen – for the foreseeable future, were it not for diesel, millions of us would starve to death within weeks.

The same goes for the relatively small fraction which is used as marine bunker fuel. As we discovered to our cost in the second half of 2021, when the economies of the world emerged from lockdown, without the steady conveyance of goods and materials across the world's shipping routes, economies experience shortages and prolonged disruptions, such as the stubborn inflation which has plagued western economies ever since.

Although it has a more discretionary role, aviation also allows for perishable goods to be moved around the planet rapidly enough to allow consumption far beyond what would be possible without global transportation. Consider that, when I was growing up in the 1960s, one of the first things you would ask when you went into the grocer's shop was "what do you have in?" This was because post-war Britain still relied on locally produced seasonal food. I was in my late teens when the first supermarket opened in the UK, and in my early twenties when the first one opened in my city. Nevertheless, by the time I was 30, seasonality was no longer an issue, and it was not uncommon to find fruit and vegetables which had been flown in from Africa or South America just hours before. This, by the way, is one of the great ironies of our age – never before did we enjoy *access to* as healthy a diet... and never before did we eat so much junk.

In saying that oil is what powers the modern world, what we really mean is that these middle (diesel and kerosene) and heavy (marine bunker oil) distillates provide the essential energy required by the global economy. Consider the ubiquitous smartphone as a proxy for the millions of products consumed across the global economy (Fig 7).

Without the ability to mine and transport minerals from around the planet to factories in East Asia, and then to transport the finished phones to consumers around the planet, the fact that we might technically "know" how to make a smartphone would be irrelevant. To consume smartphones in practice, we simply have to have access to those middle and heavy distillates. And to have them at an affordable price, oil products simply must be consumed in massive quantities... which is where petrol (gasoline) comes in.

Much of the current UK debate around "Net Zero" concerns whether we should do away with petrol-powered vehicles. Proponents argue that with better urban planning, we could reduce the need for mobility, especially if we invested heavily in modern mass transit. And by making towns and cities friendlier and safer for pedestrians

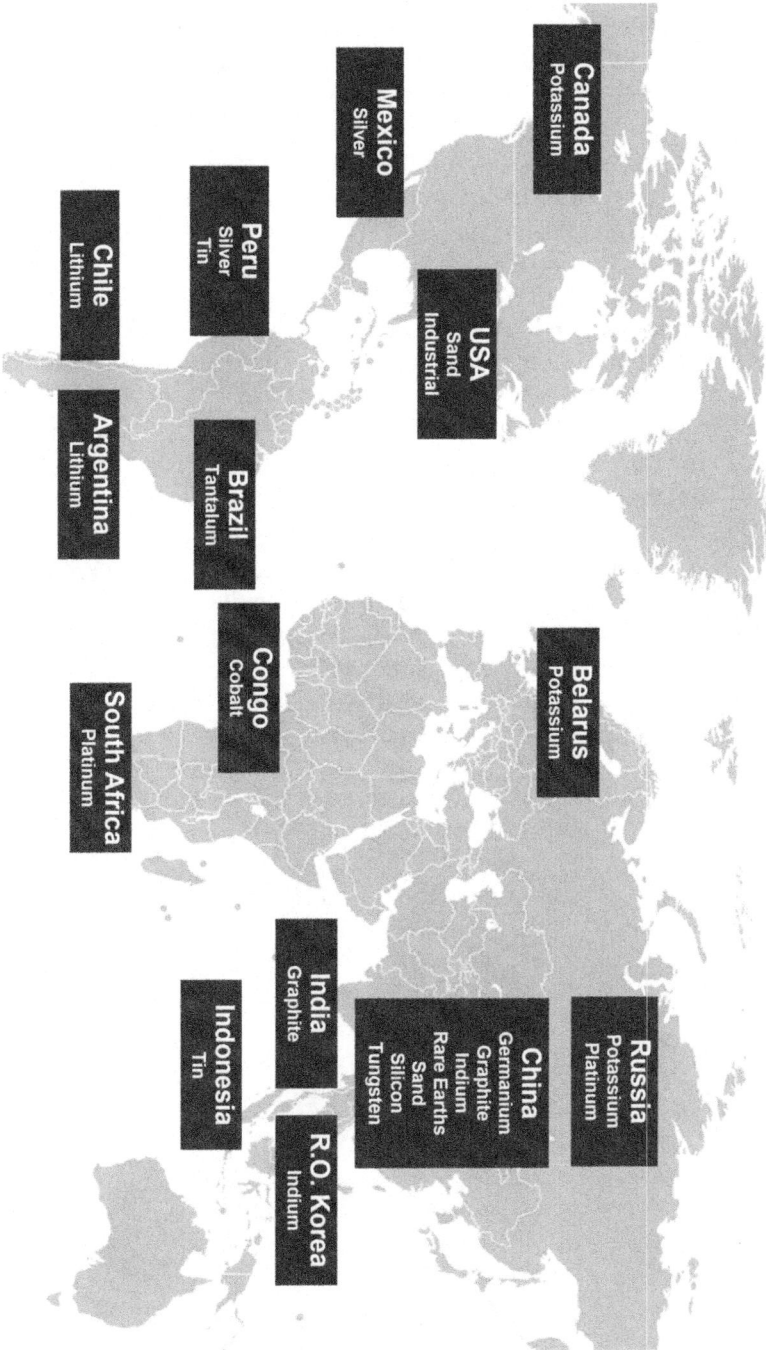

Figure 7: smartphone mineral content and sources

45

and cyclists, we could curb car use to a large extent. Opponents tend to fall back on the reality of urban decay, potholed roads and under-invested public transport which is barely fit for purpose. Moreover, while a large proportion of petrol car use might, in an ideal world, be unnecessary, petrol-powered mid-range vans remain an essential part of the transport system – resolving the "last mile" problem which bedevils road and rail haulage.

In a sense, this Net Zero debate misses the key point – unless we have a replacement for the middle and heavy distillates, then reducing petrol consumption merely turns a profitable fuel into another waste product, while making those essential fuels even more expensive. That is, mass consumption of petrol acts as a subsidy for the essential fuels. And while refineries could – at huge cost – be reconfigured to produce slightly more diesel and condensates and slightly less petrol, we would still be left with massive volumes of petrol for which the global economy has no alternative use. So, what are we going to do with it? Burn it? Dump it in landfill? Pour it into the rivers, seas and oceans? And exactly which of the millions of tons of essential and discretionary goods and resources we take for granted are we prepared to forego if we have to curb our diesel use accordingly?

Chapter 5

Oil in the modern economy (2: feedstock)

Although oil is most obviously consumed as an energy source, around 10 percent of an average barrel is used as chemical feedstocks by the global petrochemicals industry. Take a look around your home or workplace, and the odds are that every product you can see will contain at least one petrochemical. The list of products is so large that it is impossible to provide a comprehensive list or diagram. However, the top ten petrochemical products are:

- Ethylene – which is used in films, plastics, detergents and lubricants
- Benzene – which is used to make nylon fibres which are common in clothing
- Medical resins – used to purify pharmaceuticals and as a base for some cancer treatments
- Medical Plastics – everything from syringes and catheter tubes to urine bottles
- Food Preservatives – also flavour enhancers and food colourings
- Cosmetics – everything from aftershave to shampoo
- Fertilizers, herbicides and insecticides – without which modern farming yields would be significantly and dangerously lower
- Carpets and floor coverings
- Safety Glass
- Crayons and Markers.

These charts (Fig 8 & 9) from Canada's energy regulator[15] give a flavour of just how important petrochemicals are, and just how common they are in our daily lives.

We can argue about whether or which of these products is essential or discretionary, but as with petrol, this would miss the point. It is the mass market in petrochemicals which allows something as technically unnecessary as a plastic straw or a bottle of aftershave to cross subsidise something as lifesaving as a drug for cancer or an anaesthetic for open-heart surgery.

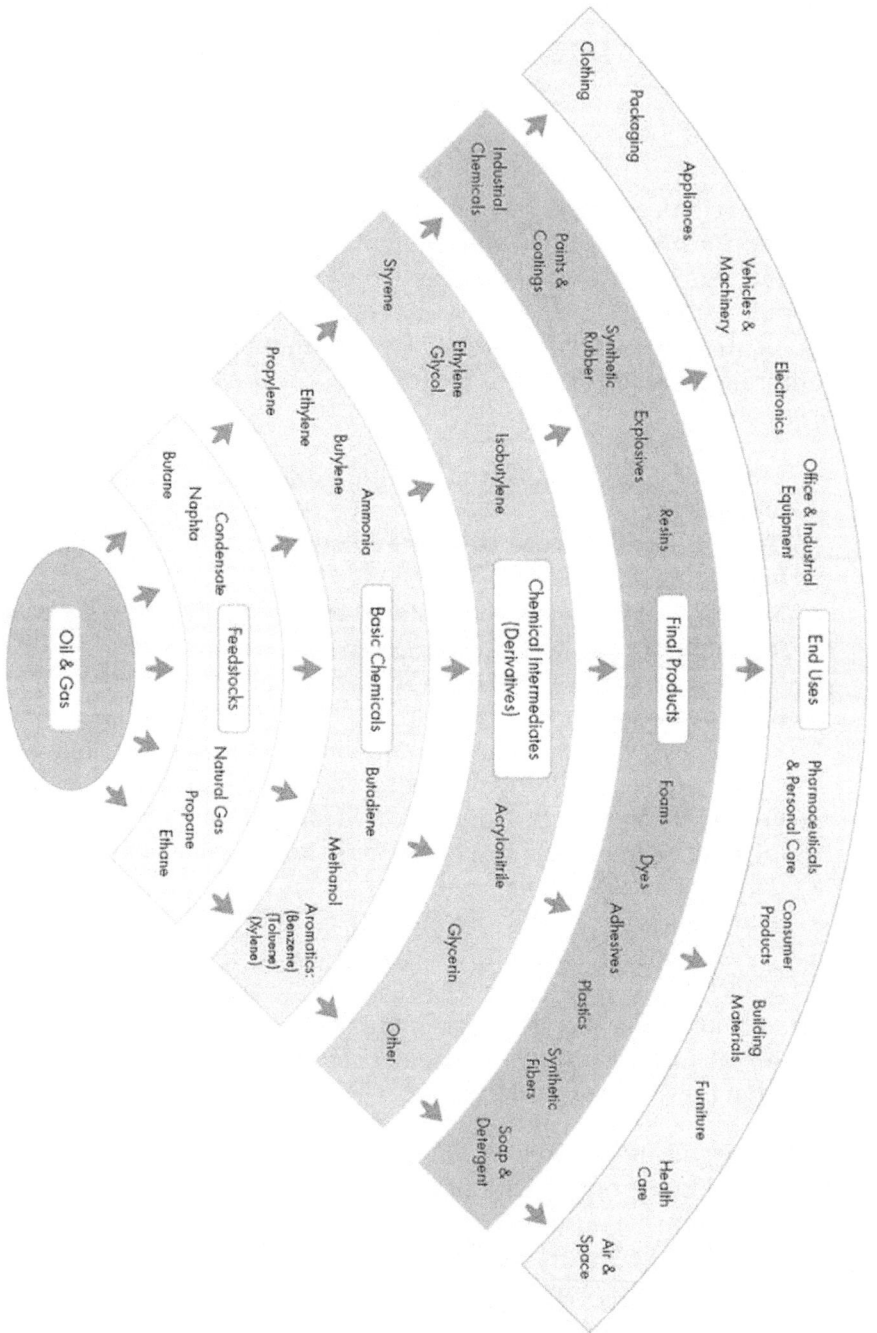

Figure 8: From oil to oil-based products

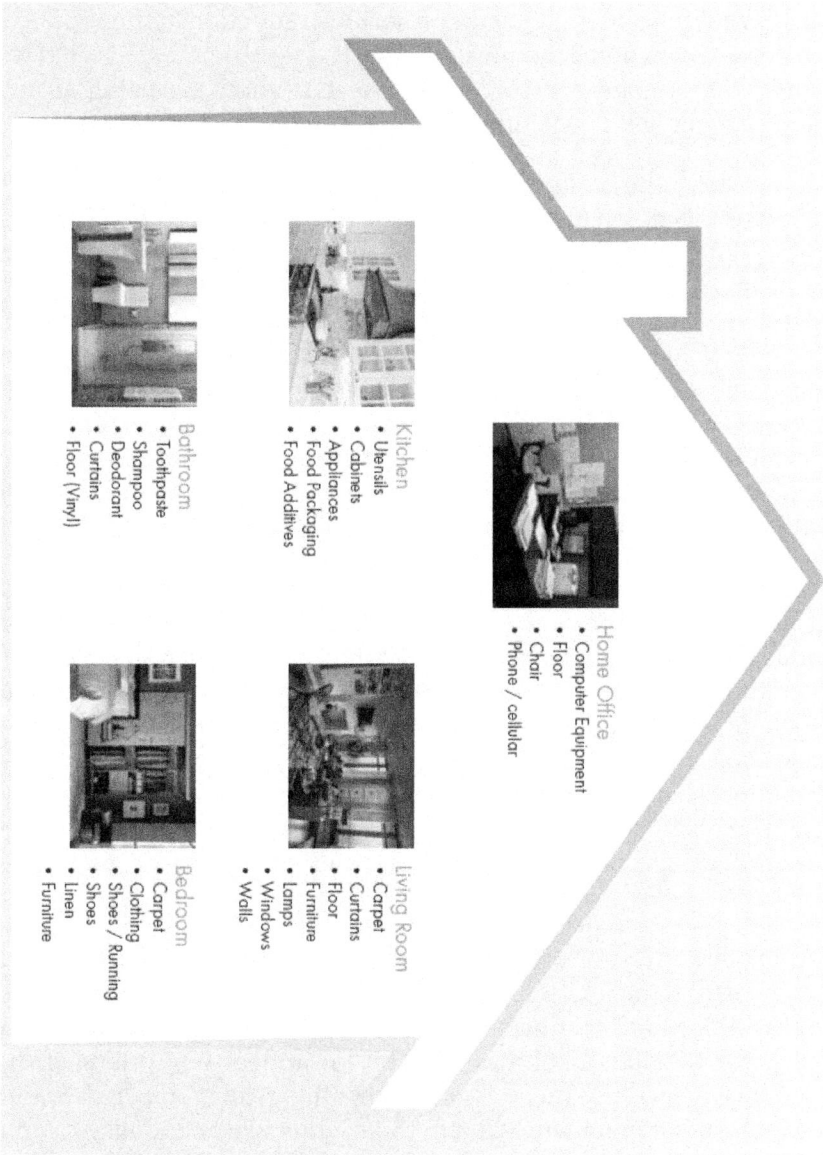

Figure 9: Oil-based products around the home

Moreover, even those things which we might technically list as non-essential, such as carpets, cheap plumbing and dental anaesthetic, certainly make modern life far more bearable than would otherwise be the case. All but the most fanatical "deep green" environmentalists would doubtless vote against any politician or party which threatened to make a serious reduction in the products we derive from petrochemicals. And yet this, ultimately, is what we would have to agree to if we were serious about lowering our oil (and coal and gas) consumption.

All too often, the debate about carbon reduction, in western states at least, boils down to "make someone else stop doing what they are doing, but don't stop me consuming the petroleum products which make my life better." But that's the hard reality – we cannot selectively reduce petrochemical products any more than we can just get rid of petrol but keep the diesel that we need to feed eight billion people. It just doesn't work that way... the only realistic option – at current levels of energy and technology – is to reduce oil consumption as a whole. And it is far from clear that a debt-based economy which depends upon continuous growth can even do this without the entire global economy entering an unstoppable collapse.

This gets to the heart of the peak oil problem – we must keep growing to prevent our life support systems (agriculture, essential industry, transport, etc.) from collapsing, but we must find a way of sustaining growth without burning fossil fuels (and no such way is available at our current level of technology and energy) and in any case, our ability to keep growing the oil production on which economic growth depends, is getting harder with each passing year. And if, as has happened since 2019 – albeit for artificial reasons – oil production falters, economic volatility invariably accompanies it.

Importantly, as our economies fall foul of debt-traps, supply shocks and energy crunches, options – such as green energy transitions or multi-billion-dollar nuclear fusion experiments – which only *appeared* to offer a solution, rapidly disappear as a mass of the population becomes more concerned with putting food on the table and at least keeping one room in their home warm enough to stave off hypothermia. Something that looked like a problem (something which can be solved) is looking more like a predicament (something we just have to live with) with each passing year as we discover that we can neither live with oil nor live without it.

Chapter 6

Are we running out of oil?

One of the barriers to understanding peak oil is a confusion about what we mean when we use the phrase "running out of oil." To give an example of what I mean, imagine that you have just filled up your car and are driving away from the filling station. If someone were to say that you are "running out of fuel," you would likely dismiss them as an idiot... how can you be running out of fuel when you have a full tank? Technically though, you *are* running out, insofar as with each mile you travel there will be less fuel than there was before. And eventually, if you were to keep driving for long enough without finding somewhere to refill, you would indeed run out.

In common sense terms though – at least for the time being – it is safe to assume that when your fuel gauge approaches the red, you will be able to find another filling station to refill your tank. It is also safe to assume that the thousands of filling stations across your country will have ongoing supplies from oil refineries which, in turn, will have regular supplies from tankers and pipelines which connect them to oil fields and oil wells around the world.

So far, so good. For most people, the only issue with oil concerns the environmental impacts of using it. Burning it as a fuel releases carbon dioxide and nitrous oxide into the atmosphere, contributing to climate change. And then there is the plastic pollution which results from using oil as a chemical feedstock. We might also add the impact of agricultural run-off on the rivers, seas, and oceans. Whatever, the one thing most people are *not* worried about is running out of oil. Indeed, the best estimates are that we are not even halfway through the Earth's oil deposits. According to Jon Jones at the University of Aberdeen[16], since 1850 we have collectively consumed 944 billion barrels of oil, while there are some 1.735 trillion barrels remaining[17].

So, no problem then? Not so fast. Back in 1850, the only use for oil was to refine kerosene as a replacement for the whale oil which used to be used for lighting – the American whaling industry having depleted the Atlantic whale populations. Only later were light and medium distillates used in the internal combustion engines which had been patented decades earlier. And it was not until the end of

Oil production

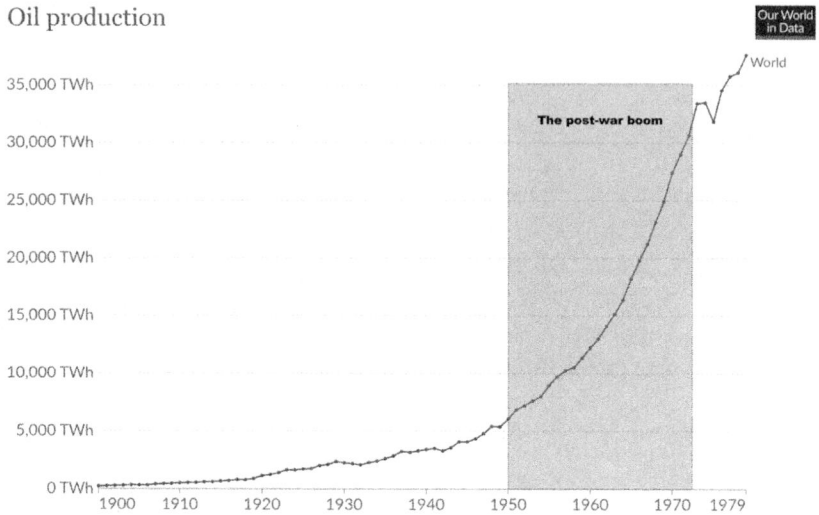

The post-war boom

World

35,000 TWh
30,000 TWh
25,000 TWh
20,000 TWh
15,000 TWh
10,000 TWh
5,000 TWh
0 TWh

1900   1910   1920   1930   1940   1950   1960   1970 1979

Figure 10: Exponential oil growth in the post-war boom years

Oil production

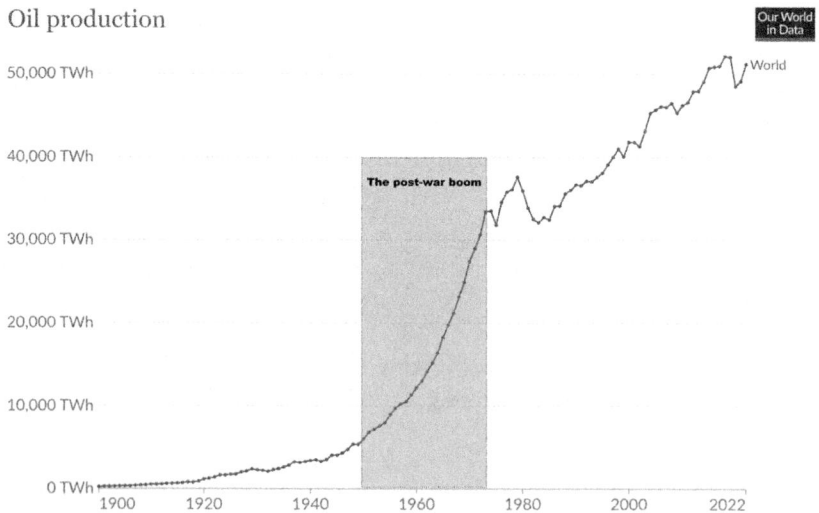

The post-war boom

World

50,000 TWh
40,000 TWh
30,000 TWh
20,000 TWh
10,000 TWh
0 TWh

1900   1920   1940   1960   1980   2000   2022

Figure 11: From boom to bust - more oil, but at a slower growth rate

the Second World War that global oil use really took off. The two decades, 1953-1973 saw oil production rise exponentially (Fig 10).

Following the oil shocks of the 1970s, oil production continued to grow – but never again exponentially. Indeed, we have produced more oil in the last thirty years than in the century and a half which preceded them (Fig 11).

At current rates of consumption, the remaining 1.735 trillion barrels will be gone in less than 50 years. More worryingly, the 1.735 trillion barrels of claimed reserves may turn out to be over-estimated. As Roger Bentley[18] explains:

> "The widely accepted global proved oil reserves are those published by organisations such as the US EIA, OPEC, *Oil and Gas Journal*, *World Oil* and BP's *Statistical Review of World Energy*; and then copied into websites including *Our World in Data*, *Worldometer* and *Statista*. These reserves data are those generally provided by the governments of the oil-producing countries concerned, and so are considered 'official data'.
>
> By contrast, Rystad Energy's proved oil reserves estimate is very much lower for two main reasons: In the 1980s, the proved oil reserves declared by some OPEC producers became significantly overstated as they competed for production quotas based partly on the size of proved reserves. More recently, large quantities of the non-conventional oils of Canada's tar sands and Venezuela's Orinoco oil have been counted as proved, even though Rystad states that most of this oil should not be classed as 'proved' under the standard oil industry definition."

The shorthand for what is going on here is the old saying, "don't count your chickens until they've hatched." Proven oil is that which can be profitably extracted at the current price. So that, if prices go up or down, the quantity of proven reserves will fluctuate accordingly even though there is no difference in the quantity of oil beneath the ground. So that, as Bentley argues, we should also include "probable reserves" – which might be proven if the price rises or if technological improvements make them profitable – together with new discoveries – which are being made continuously.

Herein though, are two additional features of peak oil. The first is that, while oil consumption has continued to rise, the peak of oil discoveries by volume was in 1964. And by the early 1980s we were consuming more oil than we were discovering. Data from Rystad Energy showed that by 2019 we were consuming 7.7 times more oil than we were discovering[19]. Although fracking in the USA filled the gap between supply and demand in the 2010s, this was not newly discovered oil. And so, rather like the driver who recently filled the tank, we were drawing down a reserve that could not later be replaced.

The second feature is price. The widely held – and wrong – view among economists was that as demand for oil outstripped supply, the price would have to rise. Indeed, it was this view which caused investors to throw good money after bad into the US shale patch. When oil prices rose to a record high in 2008, the common assumption was that we would see a sustained price of $200 per barrel by 2020. Instead, demand for oil collapsed in the post-2008 recession, causing prices to fall below $40 per barrel... leaving many shale companies unprofitable as a consequence.

In 2023, a price of $80 is about the highest that the world economy can bear. Any more than this and the recessionary pressures result in a drop in demand which forces prices down again. This is a big headache for oil producers who have drilled their way through the easiest deposits and now find themselves having to invest more and more money to produce less and less oil in return. This points to an economic limit separate from geological and technological limits. That is, even if we know the oil is there, and even if we have the technology to allow us to extract it *in theory*, if it costs more to extract it than the economy can afford, then it is going to stay in the ground forever.

There is one final, and far less obvious issue concerning the amount of oil remaining to us. This is the thermal content. As we have seen, it is the middle distillates refined from crude oil which are the lifeblood of the modern industrial economy. We might, for example, find relatively easy ways of cutting down on our consumption of petrol (gasoline) such as electric vehicles, better public transport, bicycles and better urban planning. But it is far harder to do this with the diesel which powers most of our *essential* transportation and critical infrastructure. As Alice Friedemann said of the US economy[20], when the trucks stop running, the western way of life is over:

> "Consider just how dependent we are on abundant and affordable oil, which fuels commercial transportation: Grocery stores, service stations, hospitals, pharmacies, restaurants, construction sites, manufacturers, and many other businesses receive several deliveries a day. Since they keep very little inventory, most would run out of goods within a week. When trucks stop, over 685,000 tons of garbage piles up every day in the U.S., sewage treatment ends as storage tanks fill up, and in two to four weeks water supplies would be imperiled as purification chemicals were no longer delivered. That is just the tip of the iceberg."

The problem is that the geological conditions – pressure and heat – required to produce the best oil for middle distillates turn out to be those which produced the cheap and easy deposits that we drilled and exhausted first. Shale along with deeper conventional deposits tend to deliver lighter oil which is harder and more expensive to convert to middle distillates. So that, as geologist Art Berman has shown[21], while the raw quantity of oil being produced has almost returned to the 2018 peak, the thermal content of the "oil" is in steep decline:

> "The good news is that U.S. oil production has recovered to pre-pandemic levels. The bad news is that only 60% of it is really oil... The rest is non-petroleum and comes from natural gas, corn & refinery gain... Tight oil is fine for making kerosene, jet fuel and gasoline. It cannot, however, be used for producing diesel without blending it with heavier oils, and diesel is the main cash product and workhorse of the modern global economy...

> "What I am describing is not a model. Oil quality has decreased, production decline rates have increased, and long-term secular prices are higher. Those are facts, not theory."

Berman refers to this as a "stealth peak," since while total production may yet bounce back above the 2019 level, for the global economy as a whole. But it is the middle distillates which remain irreplaceable for powering *essential* transport, without which global supply chains would rapidly collapse. And – as we witnessed during two years of lockdown, this can lead to unpredictable shortages of key components which can then cause whole sectors of the economy to slow or even cease operations.

Like the driver who recently filled the tank, the global economy still has mileage left in it. But as the diesel fuel quietly depletes, the needle is pointing closer to empty than it is full. And it is far from clear that we will be able to afford the asking price when we finally need a refill.

Chapter 7

The economy *really* does matter

In the aftermath of the 2008 crash, Queen Elizabeth II paid a visit to the econometrics clerissy at the London School of Economics, where she asked the not unreasonable question, "why did no one see it coming?" To which the assembled luminaries could do nothing but bow their heads, shuffle their feet, and murmur something about black swans.

The late Queen was misinformed though. Plenty of people had seen it coming. It is just that they were people from disciplines other than economics or, in a handful of cases, heretical economists outside the mainstream neoclassical school. What the Queen might have done inadvertently, was to restate the truth behind the old joke about economic forecasting – that it only exists to make weather forecasters appear competent. Beneath the sardonic humour, is a problem with what we – including economists – think that the economy is. This was exposed to some extent in the spring of 2020, when people around the world learned for the first time in the industrial era, what locking down whole swathes of the global economy meant. In the UK in the weeks before the first lockdown, media commentators began accusing anyone who warned about the economic consequences, of "putting profits ahead of saving lives." But as I wrote at the time[22]:

> "Unfortunately, most people – including *Guardian* commentators – have been conditioned to believe that something called 'the economy' exists separate to their/our daily lives. The economy, we assume, is something to do with central banks and stock markets, interest rates and government spending. In reality, these are just the over-complex crud that floats to the top of a global economy that is really about the complex and self-organising global networks of extraction, supply, manufacturing and transportation of everything that we consume from the clean water that comes out of the tap and the food that miraculously arrives on supermarket shelves to the gas that powers our electricity grid and the petroleum that fuels our transport."

In this way, the economy is the sum total of everything eight billion humans do, day-in, day-out. But rather than seeing the essential flows of energy and materials between people – whether as individual consumers or incorporated into businesses – economics is based only around the infinite supply of currency borrowed into existence merely as a claim on that energy and those material goods and resources.

This gives rise to the fundamental contradiction in economics – it assumes infinite growth on a planet which is incapable of providing the energetic and resource base to allow for it. As Frederick Soddy, writing during the Great Depression observed:

> "Simple contradictions of this character may serve to show that in attempting to avoid the difficulties of his subject by regarding it merely as a science of market exchanges, the economist has effectually impaled himself upon the horns of a very awkward dilemma. It may justly be asked whether it is a science of wealth, or the want of it, which leads to such curious inversions."

This, perhaps, is why so many of the "experts" manage to get things consistently wrong. Because their forecasting and prescriptions are not rooted in the real world, but on unworldly econometric models so riddled with untested assumptions that they might just as well be made up. Which is why, for example, just weeks before the 2008 crash – the biggest crisis since the Great Depression – central bankers were assuring us that there were no economic headwinds to concern us.

There is great danger for the unwary here though. Establishing that economics is little more than an ideological justification of the obscene inequality which has grown over the last half century, and that economists are less reliable than snake oil salesmen, it is all too easy to think that the economy itself doesn't matter. It was, for example, precisely this type of thinking which allowed the public health professionals and their Big Pharma backers to impose widespread business closures and house arrests in response to the pandemic, without feeling the need to consider the economic consequences. Consequences, that is, that we are now experiencing in the form of steep rises in energy prices, a cost-of-living crisis and a globally-synchronised dollar deflation... Currency might only be a claim upon the real world. But when it runs short, it is as if a lifeforce has left the human realm. As Charles Eisenstein observed[23] in the aftermath of the 2008 debacle:

"It is hugely ironic and hugely significant that the one thing on the planet most closely resembling the forgoing conception of the divine is money. It is an invisible, immortal force that surrounds and steers all things, omnipotent and limitless, an 'invisible hand' that, it is said, makes the world go 'round...

"What we call recession, an earlier culture might have called 'God abandoning the world.' Money is disappearing, and with it another property of spirit: the animating force of the human realm. At this writing, all over the world machines stand idle. Factories have ground to a halt; construction equipment sits derelict in the yard; parks and libraries are closing; and millions go homeless and hungry while housing units stand vacant and food rots in the warehouses. Yet all the human and material inputs to build the houses, distribute the food, and run the factories still exist. It is rather something immaterial, that animating spirit, which has fled. What has fled is money. That is the only thing missing, so insubstantial (in the form of electrons in computers) that it can hardly be said to exist at all, yet so powerful that without it, human productivity grinds to a halt."

Serious though it is, the well-known impact of a currency shortage is less important than the reason *why* currency shortages happen to begin with. In Chapter One, we saw how banks create currency when they make loans, and that almost all of the currency in circulation is "bank credit" – the numbers which appear on your bank statement. And so, to maintain the amount of currency in circulation *and* to pay off outstanding interest, the rate of lending must not fall. But nobody forces us – businesses or households – to take on extra debt (at least not yet). Rather, we borrow currency to buy things. Retail businesses, for example, might have a line of credit for purchasing new inventory, while a household might borrow to buy a house, a car, or a new refrigerator.

In a healthy economy, this would be happening day-in, day-out. And ordinarily banks would compete for business by maintaining a balance between the interest demanded of borrowers and the interest paid to savers. In the years preceding a crash though, this breaks down. Banks tighten their lending standards – making fewer loans and only to businesses and households with the very best credit ratings. At the same time, businesses and households may seek to limit their spending and to pay off outstanding debt.

But nobody just does this for the sake of it. This is where the financial and the material economies interface. Businesses and households borrow when they feel positive about the economy. And in those circumstances, banks are also confident about lending – the odds of defaults are low, while more potential borrowers mean more income from interest. If, on the other hand, *something* makes banks less willing to lend, and borrowers less keen on taking on debt, credit dries up and the amount of currency in circulation falls, causing a recession or something far worse.

Consider the events of October 1929. On 24 October 1929, the Dow Jones Industrial Average fell by 11 percent. On 28 October it fell by a further 12.8 percent, and another 11.7 percent on 29 October – "Black Tuesday." But it didn't end there. The years prior to the crash had seen a speculative bubble in which people borrowed to buy shares, so that the collective buying drove up the price of shares far above the value of the companies which issued them. Whether insider dealing was responsible for the crash or whether it was simply that enough investors saw that they could make money by selling at the high point and then re-buying at a lower price, is moot. The fact is that once people started heading for the exits, the system crashed. And the knock-on effect was even more catastrophic, since savers headed to the banks to try to get their money out before bad debts caused the banks to fail. And as with the stock market crash, this became self-fulfilling because – as we have seen – banks only keep a tiny fraction of deposits in the vault.

With banks failing, the remaining banks ceased lending and attempted to build their own cash reserves. So that businesses lost their access to credit, and they too began to fail. And so, the "Great Depression" of the 1930s spread not just across the USA, but through Europe and Asia, among other things creating the conditions for the Second World War... which inadvertently brought the depression to an end.

Why though, did that speculative bubble inflate to begin with? In short, the First World War. When the European powers began the war, they assumed it was going to be quick. Kaiser Wilhelm II famously declaring that it would be over "before the leaves have fallen from the trees." The British government, meanwhile, assumed that the purchase of war materials from the USA would cost around

$50 million in total... by 1917, having to supply France and Russia as well, US orders were costing $80 million *per week*!

On paper, the British and French Empires grew to their largest extent after the war, having swallowed up the former colonies of the collapsed German and Ottoman Empires. Financially, however, they were close to bankruptcy. Although everyone was too polite to formally say so, another consequence of the Great Depression was that the British defaulted on their debt to the USA in 1934[24] – which was a major reason for the American Neutrality Act of 1935 (and subsequent revisions) which left the UK unable to secure American military supplies when war broke out again in 1939.

Whereas a newly enriched America experienced the decade following the First World War as "the roaring twenties," the war-exhausted European states experienced economic stagnation and social unrest. In the East, revolution spread, while in the west, trades union militancy paved the way for social democratic and Labour parties to come to the fore. In Britain, troops mutinied and the "Triple Alliance" of dockers, miners and transport workers came close to overthrowing the government in 1919. And while the democracies did not succumb to revolution, economies had barely recovered from the First war by the time the Second was in sight.

In the USA, the influx of currency during the war helped to kickstart an economy which was far smaller than its potential. And so, instead of generating inflation, the excess currency could be invested. And in the early days, as industries boomed and everyone seemed to be richer, the boom became self-reinforcing. So long as there was spare industrial capacity, investors could keep the currency rolling. Unemployment fell and incomes rose, allowing the USA to emerge as the world's first consumer economy.

So, here's the thing almost everyone missed about the 1920s. Globally, the economy was still coal-powered. And even though the USA had begun its journey to oil dominance, much of its industrial base continued to depend upon coal too. The US peak of coal-powered coal production came in 1926 (having fallen and recovered from an earlier peak in 1918)(Fig 12).

Coal production continued to slump through 1928. And the small increase in production in 1929 was not enough to restore industrial

Coal production

4,000 TWh

3,000 TWh

United States

2,000 TWh

1,000 TWh

0 TWh
1900   1905   1910   1915   1920   1925   1933

Source: Energy Institute Statistical Review of World Energy (2023); The Shift Data Portal
OurWorldinData.org/fossil-fuels/ • CC BY

Figure 12: US coal production 1900 to 1933

fortunes. Crucially, the slump in coal production led to a spike in prices which fed into a recession (Fig 13).

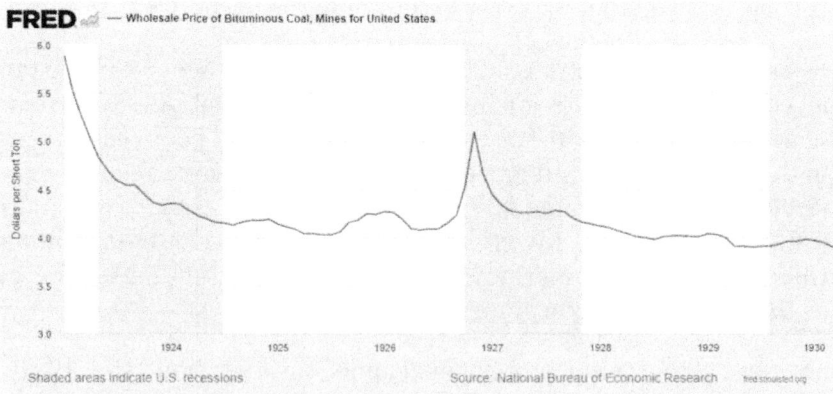

FRED — Wholesale Price of Bituminous Coal, Mines for United States

6.0

5.5

5.0

Dollars per Short Ton

4.5

4.0

3.5

3.0

1924   1925   1926   1927   1928   1929   1930

Shaded areas indicate U.S. recessions   Source: National Bureau of Economic Research   fred.stlouisfed.org

Figure 13: The spike which burst the roaring twenties bubble

In a coal-powered economy, the price of coal multiplies across the economy as the cost of everything made from, made with, or transported using coal increases too. And in the above chart, we also see proof of the old adage that "the answer to high prices is high prices." Unless there is sufficient potential demand in the wider economy to absorb the higher prices, then business and household consumption falls. And once it has fallen, the price of energy must fall accordingly. By the end of 1928, the price of coal was back to its 1926 level... but not because output had grown, but because the economy had fallen into recession and demand remained flat.

Why should the price of coal suddenly spike upward? There are two reasons – one obvious, the other hidden but important. The first is a simple shortage. Coal seams deplete, so too do mines. And if seams and mines deplete faster than new ones can be discovered and brought into production, then shortages will occur. Of course, some shortages are artificially created, for example, in 1926 Welsh miners went on strike limiting *global* production.

The second, and more obscure, reason for a shortage is that *the energy cost* of production rises too high. In preindustrial economies, most people had worked – directly or indirectly – in the production of food. But as the industrial economy developed, ever more people could be released from food production and drafted into the new urban centres where manufacturing was taking off. By the time of the Great Depression in the USA, just a quarter of the population remained in agriculture (today it is around two percent). In effect, first coal and later oil had replaced human labour in agriculture. But coal comes at a cost. Miners have to be fed and clothed. Mining equipment must be purchased and maintained. Mines themselves must be kept in good working condition. All of this feeds into the *energy cost of energy*, and it must be paid before we may enjoy the wider non-energy sectors of the economy.

Costs can be lowered by such things as economies of scale and productivity improvements. These though, tend to follow an "S" curve, with the cheap and easy improvements coming at the beginning and only the expensive and difficult ones remaining as we approach the end. The same goes for the energy source itself – nobody was going to do deep mining when coal seams were still jutting out of the sides of Welsh hills, or when deposits could be dug out from just a few metres below the ground. Related to this is the quality of the coal – there are big differences in the "thermal content" – the amount of energy which can be harnessed – between different grades of coal. Anthracite, for example, has nearly twice the thermal content of Lignite (brown coal) with Bituminous coal lying between the two.

The energy cost of energy from a new source, then, may fall dramatically in its early phase before gradually increasing as the cheap and easy deposits deplete. For the wider economy, the rising energy cost of energy causes the non-energy economy to shrink as there is less energy to go around, and ever more is required just to secure today's and tomorrow's energy (Fig 14).

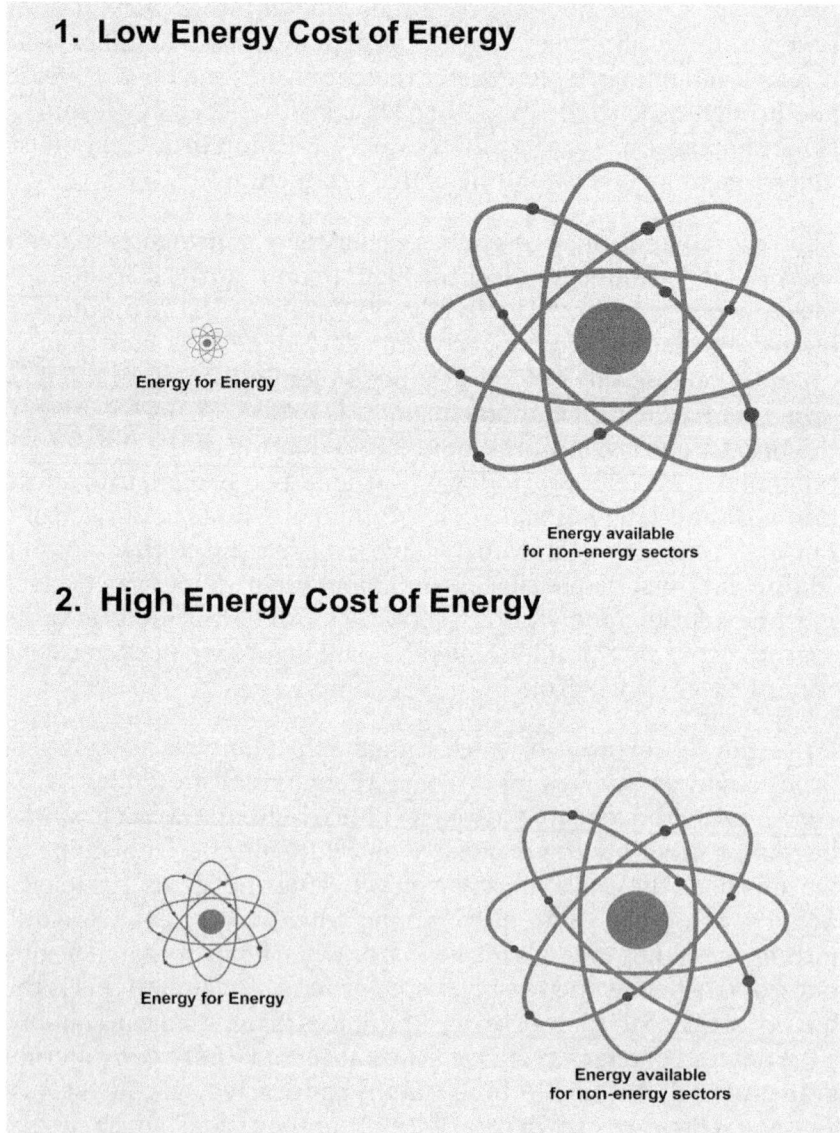

1. Low Energy Cost of Energy

Energy for Energy

Energy available
for non-energy sectors

2. High Energy Cost of Energy

Energy for Energy

Energy available
for non-energy sectors

Figure 14: Energy cost of energy and the economy

Remember how we saw that an average ton of coal provides the equivalent of 5.5 years of human labour? That worked out at around £184,000 at today's average wage, for which we paid just £11.80. Now, suppose the energy cost of energy were to double. This would entail a loss of £92,000 per ton of work to the wider, non-energy economy. Of course, in something as complex as an economy, it is impossible to predict exactly where that loss would be experienced. Although we might anticipate that the majority of the loss would be in discretionary sectors rather than in essentials like food and shelter. We might also anticipate that – not understanding what was happening – companies would look at their biggest cost – wages – in an attempt to claw back some of the loss. This might involve a hard wage cut – including lay-offs – or a soft cut in which wages rise at below the rate of inflation.

This brings us to the part of the story that Marx got right... although he mislabelled it a "crisis of over-production." By cutting workers' wages, and even by laying off workers entirely, companies might be able to temporarily offset the rising energy cost of energy. But because the loss of wages translates into a loss of consumption, companies can no longer pass the higher energy costs onto consumers. Thus, what actually happens is a "crisis of under-consumption," which, in the modern world results in a "crisis of under-borrowing."

One possible response to this is for governments to create and distribute new currency. But this is extremely dangerous unless there is a high volume of untapped and cheap energy with which to absorb the additional currency. To inject additional currency when the economy has already stalled, risks generating monetary inflation on top of the recessionary slowdown. Another – equally dangerous – response is for governments to implement austerity measures... raising taxes and cutting public spending. This though, serves only to compound the problem by withdrawing even more currency from circulation – in effect, lowering inflation by shrinking the economy.

Notice that the first response is broadly the prescription offered by parties and activists on the left, while the second response is the one preferred by the right. Which should further reinforce the widely held view that politicians are clueless when it comes to economic crises. It is also why, in times of profound energy-based crises, we tend to see the rise of opportunist political extremism which offers unorthodox – and generally wrong – alternatives to the failed "solutions" offered by left and right.

Factoring "peak coal-based coal" into the story of the 1929 crash and the ensuing depression, we might, then, have the basis of a hypothesis based around energy rather than the idiocy of politicians and economists and the fickle practices of financial speculators:

- We experience a spike in the cost of primary energy, causing the energy price to spike.
- Over a period of two or three years, this higher price spreads and multiplies through the economy.
- In response, companies seek to raise prices and/or cut costs by cutting wages or laying off workers.
- This leads to a further decline in consumption which begins to show up in economic data.
- Investors (including banks and financial institutions) who depend upon a growing economy begin to notice the slowdown and the more alert among them begin to withdraw from financial markets.
- At the same time, banks begin to tighten lending standards to decrease their exposure to defaults. This results in less currency in circulation, further depressing the economy.
- The promised "permanent" increase in the value of assets turns out to be transitory after all, and despite various interventions to try to shore up the markets, panic ensues.
- We then discover that what we would today call the shadow banking sector had been devising all manner of unsustainable means of making money in Ponzi fashion.

The knock-on in 1929 was that ordinary people across the USA realised that if the banks – where their savings were on deposit – had been making loans which were only good if the price of assets kept rising, then their savings might be wiped out. And so, queues appeared outside banks which had nowhere near enough cash to meet demand. What began, then, as a seemingly innocuous increase in the price of the primary energy source had morphed into a banking crisis. And in a debt-based economy, this meant a massive crash in "capital formation" – the ability to raise the money to fund business activity.

Notice then, that it is not the rise in the price of primary energy in and of itself which results in a prolonged depression. Rather, it is the inverted pyramid of debt-based claims on future energy, which is the greater problem since our whole way of life is based on the assumption that the real economy of energy and resources will continue to grow indefinitely. So that, when a spike in the energy cost of energy results in an unexpected slowdown, the entire financial economy can unravel, rendering the populations of industrial economies unable to function.

If coal had been the only high-density energy source on Earth, then 1929 would have marked the apex of the industrial economy. The remorseless increase in the coal-powered energy cost of coal would have forced a permanent contraction of the non-energy sectors of the economy. Ultimately, even as pockets of coal-powered production remained, urban living would have broken down as more and more people had to return to the land just to put food on the table. Indeed, during the Great Depression it was common for people to work in exchange for food rather than wages. However, the myth of infinite growth was inadvertently reinforced in the 1940s.

It was our fortune and misfortune, that an even more versatile and energy-dense fossil fuel had already begun to make an appearance prior to the 1929 crash. Although oil was initially used to produce kerosene for lighting, with heavier oil used as a lubricant, it was the development of the internal combustion engine from the 1870s and the use of oil as a replacement for coal for steam ships in the 1890s, which launched the technologies of the oil age.

Oil powered vehicles took centre stage in the 1914-1918 war, when aeroplanes and tanks were developed and improved. Less obviously, Germany, which lacked access to oil, continued to use coal power even as the Entente countries – supplied with oil from the USA – were able to use trucks and buses for moving ammunition, equipment, and troops up to the frontline. As one German general complained after the war, in the later stages of the war, when the Germans were preparing an offensive, the Entente could hear it coming weeks in advance as steam trains rattled along narrow-gauge railways used for transport to the front lines. The Entente, in contrast, were able to use relatively quiet vehicles which used rubber tyres, so that the first the Germans realised an assault was coming was when the brief preliminary artillery barrage rained down on them.

Beyond the military, automobile production and use were almost entirely an American pursuit in the years prior to the Second World War[25]. Indeed, during the depression, vehicle production slumped back to pre-1914 levels (falling again during the Second World War as production switched from civilian to military output – aeroplanes, tanks and jeeps rather than cars and buses). Outside the USA prior to the Second World War, motoring was a pursuit enjoyed mostly by the wealthy... and even this came to an end in 1939 as the need to divert imported petroleum to the military brought non-essential car use to an end.

One of our key misunderstandings of war is due to a history which tends to focus on big battles and great leaders. However, as military psychologist Norman Dixon explains[26]:

> "War is primarily concerned with two sorts of activity – the delivering of energy and the communication of information. Most combatants are involved in the former, a few – generals among them – with the latter.

> "In war, each side is kept busy turning its wealth into energy which is then delivered, free, gratis and for nothing, to the other side. Such energy may be muscular, thermal, kinetic or chemical. Wars are only possible because the recipients are ill-prepared to receive it and convert it into a useful form for their own economy. If, by means of, say, impossibly large funnels and gigantic reservoirs, they could capture and store the energy flung at them by the other side, the recipients of this unsolicited gift would soon be rich, and the other side so poor, that further warfare would be unnecessary for them and impossible for their opponent."

Energy – in the form of oil – is why the Axis powers went to war – they didn't have enough – and why the Allies prevailed. Germany had to go to the Caucasus to secure the oil it needed to have any chance of defeating the Allies. Its failure to secure Grozny or to produce oil from the briefly captured Maikop field, together with the failure at Stalingrad – which was intended to cut the Russian supply of oil along the Volga – condemned Germany to eventual defeat, because at the same time the USA was ramping up production... eventually providing six out of every seven barrels of oil consumed (with most of the rest coming from Venezuela). One consequence was that while every allied division landing in Normandy in June 1944 was motorised, nine in ten of the German divisions facing them was horse-drawn.

In the Pacific, it was the US oil embargo on Japan following the attack on French Indochina, which forced the Japanese to choose between war or decline... they chose war. But once the USA had ramped up production, the Japanese attempt to hold a static perimeter along the various Pacific atolls was doomed. As with Germany, it was only a matter of time. And while western histories focus on the eventual use of the single biggest energy munition ever used, as important to the Japanese surrender in August 1945 was the ability of an oil-powered, motorised Red Army to drive through Manchuria like a hot knife through butter – the prospect of being divided between the USA and the USSR being sufficient for a majority of the Japanese leadership to opt for the lesser evil of an entirely US occupation.

The massive increase in energy and industrial capacity unleashed during the war required a complete overhaul of the system of global trade and finance. The system developed at the Bretton Woods conference in 1944, required a massive program of dollar printing and distribution – via Marshall Aid – to prevent an international currency crisis. And contrary to economic orthodoxy the sudden access to billions of new dollars *did not* result in the anticipated inflation. The reason why is simple although obfuscated by economists' failure to understand the essential role of energy in the economy. Oil – more energy dense and versatile than the coal it was replacing – was abundant. And the additional energy derived from this cheap and abundant oil exerted significant deflationary pressure on the cost of resources and manufactured goods. That is, the newly created currency was entering an economy which – because of oil – had massive untapped potential. This is why, once the war-torn economies of Asia and Europe had completed their reconstruction, their switch from being coal-powered to oil-powered economies ushered in the two decades of exponential economic growth between 1953 and 1973... the so-called "post-war boom." As historian Paul Kennedy[27] explains:

"The accumulated world industrial output between 1953 and 1973 was comparable in volume to that of the entire century and a half which separated 1953 from 1800. The recovery of war-damaged economies, the development of new technologies, the continued shift from agriculture to industry, the harnessing of national resources within 'planned economies,' and the spread of industrialization to the Third World all helped to effect this dramatic change. In an even more emphatic way, and for much the same reasons, the volume of world trade also grew spectacularly after 1945..."

Not understanding the energetic driver behind this massive economic growth, economists and politicians began to treat it as a new normal. Indeed, even as late as the 1980s, political and economic debate revolved around the best means by which we might return to the conditions of the post-war years. But something happened in the 1970s which – while partially artificial – had a similarity to the process which unfolded in the late 1920s.

The price of oil had been trending downward throughout the 1960s, as production grew exponentially to meet an industrialising world's insatiable demand. In large part, this was due to the activities of the Texas Railroad Commission. But while this favoured the USA – and to a lesser extent, the Europeans and Japan – it was resented by former colonies of the western states which were emerging as major oil producers, but which required a higher oil price to develop their own economies. Nevertheless, so long as the USA remained the world's "swing producer," the TRC could continue to maintain the price (Fig 15).

Beginning in 1969 though, the world price of oil began to rise as non-US producers fought against attempts by the TRC to maintain control. And even *before* the OPEC oil embargo in October 1973, the oil price (adjusted for inflation) had risen back to its 1950s level.

What most people missed – and, indeed, the establishment media had mocked the idea of – was a prediction made by Marion King Hubbert coming to fruition. After 1970, the continental USA oil fields began to decline. This, in turn, meant that the TRC could no longer ramp up production to hold oil prices down. There was, in fact, something artificial about the whole thing. The oil giants *could* have done more to raise production. But since they were often the

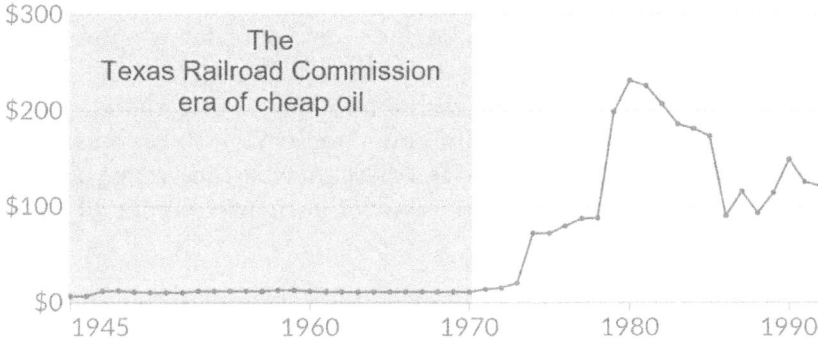

Crude oil prices

Global crude oil prices, measured in US dollars per cubic meter.

Figure 15: The TRC era of cheap oil

same corporations producing the oil on behalf of the OPEC countries, why hold down prices that they would otherwise profit from? Indeed, since – even by Hubbert's calculations – the world was decades away from peak production – the fact that US production was falling didn't seem to matter much. Except that America's weakness provided the OPEC states with an opportunity to flex their economic muscle.

The pretext was western support for Israel in the 1973 Arab-Israeli war. The OPEC states turned off the spigots, and the western economies were plunged into chaos as oil products were hard to obtain. The price of oil shot up, reflecting just how dependent upon oil the economies of the developed states had become. Indeed, it is something of an historical irony that while abundant coal had allowed the developed states to industrialise in the first place, with the exception of the USA and the Soviet Union, the developed states had little oil of their own. So that, and irrespective of the news headlines, what was happening in the 1970s was a rebalancing of energy wealth, as developed states like Britain, France, Japan and West Germany were obliged to pay more for their primary energy so that former colonies could develop their own domestic economies.

Economists drew a false conclusion from the 1973-74 oil shock – that rising oil prices are *inflationary.* This seems plausible enough, since higher oil prices metastasise across the wider economy as everything made from or transported using oil must rise in cost too. But in the late 1920s, the spike in the cost of primary energy had a *deflationary* impact on the economy, ushering in a decade of depression. What happened in the early 1970s though, was a combination of monetary inflation – not least of the excess dollars used to fund the cold war and the Vietnam war – and rising oil prices which, initially, exacerbated the inflationary impact of excess currency creation.

This is why the 1970s is thought of as a "stagflationary" decade. Currency creation served to devalue currencies – which is experienced as rising prices – while the re-adjustment of the economy to higher primary energy costs resulted in business failures and unemployment. This is a point missed by most economists, who regard all price increases as inflation. The price of goods or services can increase for material reasons – a ton of copper, for example, might be more expensive simply because the global cost of copper mining has increased (perhaps because ore grades have fallen) irrespective of how much currency is in circulation. This kind of price rise is *deflationary* because the economy must readjust to the new cost of copper – if we are obliged to spend more on copper, then we must spend less on other things. This, in turn, may result in business failures and job losses in those parts of the economy which were engaged in those other things. This is different to what happens when governments and central banks create too much currency. When this happens, the currency itself is devalued so that the price of everything measured in that currency *appears* to rise.

The saving grace in the 1970s was that there was plenty of affordable oil in the ground – only the location changed. The reign of the continental USA oil fields was at an end, the OPEC era had begun... although this was mitigated in the west by the opening of deposits off Alaska, the North Sea and the Gulf of Mexico. The spectacular exponential growth of oil production – and the accompanying boom in economic activity – between 1953 and 1973 may have come to an end, but oil production continued to increase, and the economy settled into a slower pace of growth. So that, for a brief period from the late-1980s to the mid-2000s, a degree of economic and political stability was re-established.

Notice though, that in 1929 and 1973, it was not solely the energy price spike which brought about the economic crisis. Rather, the energy price spike had occurred at a time when the financial economy was over-extended. Too much currency had been borrowed into existence both by governments and private actors, compared to the growth in the "real," material economy. In this light, the spike in the cost of primary energy served as the pin which burst a big financial bubble.

The same broad pattern occurred again from the mid-1980s. Among other things, the de-regulation of the banking and financial system in 1986 – the so-called "big bang" – gave commercial banks far greater scope to increase the volumes of currency they could spirit into existence. Prior to the big bang, in a world still haunted by the 1929 crash, banks had tended to be conservative in their approach to lending. Bank managers usually lived within the communities where they worked and had a good knowledge of the local employers along with which customers were the most reliable. It had to be this way, since the loans they issued might take 10, 20, or 30 years to be repaid. And while the bank would make a healthy profit from the interest, there was always the risk of default – an employer might go bankrupt while a homebuyer might fall sick.

By the mid-1980s, the widespread use of computers allowed banks to develop an old idea of turning the income from loans and mortgages into a savings instrument. While a bank's statisticians could predict *how many* of the loans would go bad, they couldn't predict *which ones*. But suppose, for example, they knew that three percent would go bad. Now suppose they took 100 of their loans and divided the income from each into 100 parts, and then recombined them so that they ended up with 100 instruments containing one percent of the income from each of the original 100 loans. They would now have a savings instrument – a security – which they could guarantee would repay 97 percent of the potential income. And just to be on the safe side, they could insure the income at that level. On this basis, instead of having a filing cabinet full of 30-year mortgages, the banks could immediately sell the (income from the) loans they were issuing to third party investors. That is, instead of having to wait three decades to profit from their loans,

73

the banks could profit from them within hours of issuing them… what could possibly go wrong?

It is likely that the politicians who legislated the 1986 deregulation simply assumed that bankers would continue to be a conservative force, and that borrowing would continue to be limited to the most credit-worthy businesses and households. The temptation though, proved too strong. Working people who lived through the period will remember struggling to open their front doors because of the mountain of pre-approved loans pushed through their letter boxes. The car market changed dramatically as dealers who once wanted payment in cash could now make more money selling finance deals than selling the cars. And by the beginning of the new century, local banks like the National Westminster, the Midland, and the Royal Bank of Scotland, had morphed into global behemoths turning over more currency than most of the world's developing nations. Since bank lending is the source of almost all of the currency in circulation, the massive increase in loans created an equally massive expansion in the currency supply, creating what appeared to be an economic boom… but which turned out to have been another bubble.

The early years of the twenty-first century were marked by an insanity which would have been familiar to those who lost everything in October 1929. It was the age of *The Secret*[28] where you only had to think yourself to be wealthy and wealth would surely seek you out:

> "Decide what you want to be, do, and have, think the thoughts of it, emit the frequency, and your vision will become your life."

It was a time when the houses people lived in were earning more than people's incomes, when economists proclaimed a "Great Moderation" and a "permanent plateau of prosperity," a time when almost everyone agreed that "this time is different." And then it went horribly wrong…

In the popular imagination, the 2008 crash was the result of a banking "credit crunch" brought about by the sale of sub-prime mortgages. Neither is true. The banks' claim to have a "liquidity" crisis was a lie – they did not have assets which were difficult to sell, they had a mountain of what they had thought were assets but which turned out not to be worth the paper they were printed on.

Meanwhile, sub-prime borrowers were not the cause of the crisis but rather its symptom.

So, what really happened? First, the post-big bang environment created a lending frenzy which massively inflated bank profits. But to remain profitable, banks had to keep issuing loans. The problem is that there are only so many credit-worthy borrowers, and not all of them want to borrow. And so, we reached what has been called "peak debt[29]." The only options for the banks were to accept a decline in profits or to extend loans even to people who couldn't hope to repay them.

This kind of financial situation is often likened to Wile E. Coyote running off the cliff – so long as he doesn't look down, he can keep running. But *something* caused enough people to look down prior to 2008, that the whole banking and financial sector looked set to implode. And this wasn't a solely psychological event.

In 2005, global conventional oil production peaked in the same way as conventional coal-powered coal production had peaked in 1927. In the UK this was compounded by the decline in North Sea production passing the point at which Britain became a net importer of oil and gas. As in 1927-1929 and 1971-74, the price of primary energy spiked, and this spread and multiplied across the economy. However, rather than understanding the *deflationary* impact of rising energy costs, central banks took rising prices as a sign of *monetary inflation*. And failing to understand that it was the second oil shock, following the Iranian revolution, which brought inflation down in the early 1980s, they made the mistake of adding rising interest rates to an already struggling economy.

The interest rate rises between 2006 and 2008 proved enough to tip borrowers who had previously managed to service their debts into default. And these defaults caused the whole house of cards to come tumbling down. Securities based on those loans failed, as did insurances based only on a "normal" rate of failure. But worst of all, it turned out that, in order to maintain demand for securities, the banks had been buying up what turned out to be each other's bad debt. These bad securities were the "assets" which the banks claimed still had value, when in fact they were worthless.

This raises an interesting question. If the central bankers had taken the alternative lesson – that primary energy price rises are deflationary – from the 1920s and 1970s, would the 2008 crash have been averted? We cannot know, of course. But it is likely the crisis would have unfolded in a different way. Instead of borrowers being wiped out by excessive interest rates, a period of rising prices would have been followed by business failures and rising unemployment. And because of the unsustainable levels of debt which had been built up since 1986, the same banking crisis would have followed – it would just have been different business loans and different household mortgages which went bad.

The response of central banks and governments to the crisis was far from inevitable. Nevertheless, one way or another a huge amount of bad debt was going to have to be written off. And the political argument at the time was about who would pick up the bill. The obvious – and fair – thing to have done was to have allowed the banks to go bust, have the governments nationalise the assets, and then use the power of government and central banks to create currency to recapitalise the banks – also using some of the new currency to compensate ordinary depositors and small businesses. The anticipation of something like this was on the faces of America's bank CEOs when they were ordered to the White House by the new president, Barak Obama. The smiles on their faces when they left the meeting showed that, not only were the public going to be forced to pay, but the bankers – who had caused the problem in the first place – had been put in charge of cleaning up the mess.

The central banks created currency out of thin air and used it to buy up the bad debt that was sat on bank balance sheets. And by lowering the overnight interest rate to a below inflation 0.5 percent, they created the conditions for banks to start lending again – although not on the scale prior to the crash. The big winners – other than the banks themselves – were those large, listed corporations which could access the 0.5 percent rate to borrow in order to buy back their own shares – which had been paying above inflation dividends. For ordinary investors and savers though, the new financial environment created a "search for yield." Previously "safe" savings accounts left savers out of pocket as inflation ate the value of their deposits faster than the interest paid on them. Pension funds – which require returns of five percent or more to meet their commitments – had the added burden that by law they have to hold government bonds – which, again, were paying far less than the rate of inflation (one reason why pension funds have been cutting the benefits on offer to new members).

There was an unexpected winner in this low-yield environment, however. Following the peak in conventional oil production, most economists had expected the price of oil to keep increasing, with many anticipating a price of $200 per barrel by 2020. But higher oil prices make previously unprofitable deposits appear viable. And on this basis, attention turned to the previously unprofitable practice of horizontal drilling and hydraulically fracturing the vast shale deposits in the USA.

Fracking was hyped as a revolution, although neither the technique nor the deposits were new. Nevertheless, the PR people began to talk about "Saudi America" and "the new century of energy independence." And investors lapped it up… the yields on so-called "junk bonds," like the high-risk shares in fracking companies were as good as it gets in a financial environment where everyone else was losing value. And so, investors failed to look too hard at the veracity of the promises being made by the fracking companies.

Remember how the cure for high prices is high prices, and how rising primary energy prices are actually deflationary? Well, the high oil prices of 2008 proved unsustainable because the economy couldn't bear them. And with the global economy in recession, demand for oil slumped… just at the point when the first fracked oil was coming on stream. Instead of the $150-per-barrel price promised to investors, the price of oil slumped below $50-per-barrel… and stayed there despite Saudi Arabia and Russia cutting production in an attempt to hold prices up. This partially explains the discrepancy between the value of the shale reserves fracking companies claimed to their investors and the – legally required – values reported to the US Securities and Exchange Commission (Fig 16).

Over the decade between the Crash and the Covid, there was no "Goldilocks" oil price high enough for producers but low enough for the wider economy. And so, the oil price see-sawed (Fig 17).

Selling the Shale Boom

An analysis of 73 shale drillers found that almost all reported higher oil and gas prospects to investors than to the Securities and Exchange Commission (SEC). These six companies illustrate the range of estimates within the industry.

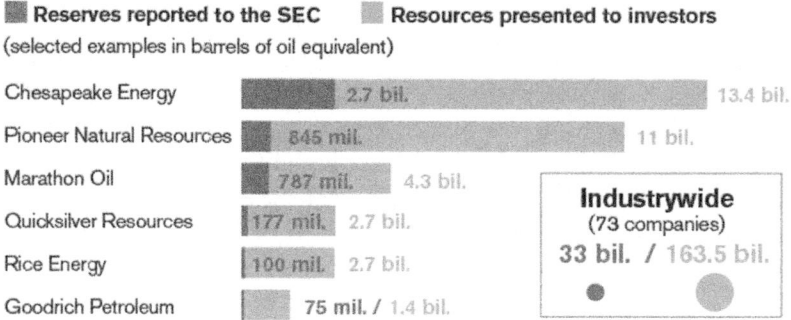

█ Reserves reported to the SEC   **█ Resources presented to investors**
(selected examples in barrels of oil equivalent)

Chesapeake Energy	2.7 bil.	13.4 bil.
Pioneer Natural Resources	845 mil.	11 bil.
Marathon Oil	787 mil. 4.3 bil.	
Quicksilver Resources	177 mil. 2.7 bil.	
Rice Energy	100 mil. 2.7 bil.	
Goodrich Petroleum	75 mil. / 1.4 bil.	

Industrywide
(73 companies)
33 bil. / 163.5 bil.
●   ⬤

Source: Company presentations and SEC filings   **Bloomberg** Visual Data

Figure 16: Selling worthless paper to chumps

Figure 17: Oil prices - what goes up must come down

Most alarmingly, despite the $75-per-barrel price in 2017 being well below the $100 during the post-crash depression, the price proved too high for the economy. Indeed, the economy was on course for another recession in 2019-20, although this was eclipsed by the impact of ill-advised economic lockdowns which were stagflationary

– i.e., both inflationary and deflationary – as a result, on the one hand of governments going on a currency creation spree, and on the other of disrupted supply and locked-in production, including of oil drilling and refining.

Left to their own devices, oil prices – at one point above $100-per-barrel again – would have – and will – cause a deflationary depression as the broader economy is forced to get by on far less energy than it had been prior to the pandemic. This though, has been eclipsed by the impact of governments spending currency like so many drunken sailors on a weekend shore leave, during a period where consumption was constrained by lockdowns. The result, when economies finally opened up in the autumn of 2021, was a spike in consumer spending which – exacerbated by supply shortages – sent prices spiralling up at rates not seen since the 1980s.

Having – correctly – seen the inflation as "temporary," the central bankers blinked. So long as governments ceased creating and handing out new "stimulus" currency, the pent-up savings from the pandemic would have been spent soon enough. And as supply chains healed, prices would have stabilised. Moreover, if the price of oil stayed high, a recession would follow, causing overall demand to fall thereby bringing prices down again. Instead, governments continued to find things to throw new currency at, and the central banks allowed themselves to be pressured into using the one tool available to them – interest rate rises – to engineer the recession that the politicians seem so reluctant to allow.

At the time of writing – Autumn 2023 – the global economy in general and the western economies in particular face a crisis far worse than in 2008. Then, the spike in the price of primary energy threatened to bring down banks. This time around, it is governments and sovereign currencies which are at risk, as international investors – institutions and individuals – doubt the ability of post-industrial and de-industrialising states like the UK and Germany to raise the tax income to repay their existing dollar-denominated debts out of increasingly energy-deprived economies that lack the necessary export-base.

As in 2008, we cannot know exactly how this will play out, since rationality is usually trumped by the shouting of those with the loudest voices and the deepest pockets. Nevertheless, we are likely in the early stages of an "economic death spiral" in which falling *surplus* energy crushes demand and forces the economy to shrink.

Chapter 8

Welcome to the Death Spiral

In the summer of 2016, Iain Conn, CEO of British Gas owner Centrica, and Vincent de Rivaz, CEO of EDF Energy called on the UK government to radically reform the way energy is priced. Unless this was done, they argued, Britain risked an "energy death spiral" which would bankrupt the entire energy supply industry. This is because of the regressive charge for infrastructure which falls disproportionately on the lowest users – generally those least able to pay. As Emily Gosden wrote in the *Telegraph*[30]:

> "About 13pc of a typical household electricity bill is made up of environmental and social levies to fund green subsidies and insulation schemes, while a further 25pc of an electricity bill consists of levies to fund network infrastructure."

The risk – particularly if energy prices rose in future – was that those on the lowest incomes would cut energy use to a bare minimum to make ends meet. But at the same time, those at the top of the income ladder could take advantage of generous subsidies for using solar panels to generate their own electricity and to supply excess electricity to the grid. As Gosden explained:

> "A household that installs solar panels – usually in return for subsidies – will buy less power from the grid and so will contribute far less to the network costs, despite being equally dependent on it when the sun doesn't shine."

This set up a situation in which the energy market faced a squeeze from both ends. Those at the top could use feed-in subsidies to fund a large part of their domestic energy consumption, while those at the bottom simply shivered in the dark. Something similar was also happening in the business sector, where the most profitable companies were deploying subsidised solar panels, wind turbines and biomass boilers, while less profitable businesses were cutting their use in an attempt to save money. The risk to the energy supply companies – which Conn and de Rivaz were raising with government – was of a loss of custom sufficient to render the companies insolvent. That is, as those at both ends opted out, the cost of running the industry would have to fall on a shrinking squeezed middle.

In a review of Britain's energy policy the following year[31], professor Dieter Helm – an expert in the economics of the energy industry – highlighted the cost of energy as a major obstacle to the environmental policies the government was trying to implement:

> "It is not particularly difficult to set out what an efficient energy system might look like which meets the twin objectives of the climate change targets and security of supply. There would, however, remain a binding constraint: the willingness and ability to pay for it. There have to be sufficient resources available, and **there has in a democracy to be a majority who are both willing to pay and willing to force the population as a whole to pay**. This constraint featured prominently in the last three general elections, and it has not gone away." (My emphasis)

Both Helm's note of caution and the warning from energy bosses was prescient for a country which had become a net importer of fossil fuels in 2005, and which was increasingly dependent upon imported electricity and (albeit indirectly via the European wholesale market) cheap Russian gas to keep its lights on. The collapse in production of all three fossil fuels in the wake of lockdown – and exacerbated by the self-destructive sanctions on Russia following the invasion of Ukraine – created precisely the storm that they had warned against. Energy prices rose to unprecedented highs, so that it wasn't just the poor who were struggling. In the winter of 2022-23 – which was mercifully mild – nearly 75 percent of UK households made cuts to their consumption despite the government spending £36bn to pay for essential energy use (in effect, a £36bn subsidy to the energy suppliers).

Even before that, rising prices since 2021 had caused hundreds of energy supply companies – which are mostly no more than billing agencies – to go broke, having offered customers far lower prices than could be sustained in the new, high price environment. The customers of the failed companies have been transferred onto far more expensive deals with the remaining companies – which tend to be the big "vertically-integrated" (i.e., energy producers and suppliers) corporations. But with wholesale prices remaining stubbornly high even as European gas and electricity supply has shrunk, prices have barely fallen for the 2023-24 winter, and there is no guarantee that, without more government support, some of the big corporations might fail.

The loss of the critical mass of consumers needed to keep the energy companies profitable is all too common in private business. At the time of writing, for example, one of the UK's biggest and long-lived discount retailers, *Wilco* has collapsed with some 400 High Street stores closing. The reasons for the collapse are not particularly difficult to understand. Supply chain problems following lockdown left stores with too many empty shelves, rent and staff costs were too high, and access to cheap credit came to an end. And while journalists blamed the company's management, it is notable that competitors – who were supposed to be leaner and meaner, only took over the 50 best located stores. The broader cost-of-living crisis making the remaining stores – mostly in the ex-industrial, rundown seaside and small-town regions of the UK – unviable even for corporations with a track record of rescuing failing businesses.

The difference is that where one discount retailer fails, there are three or four competitors on hand to maintain supply to the customer base. And so, while the loss of *Wilco* is bad news for its former employees and its owners, and while a few of us see it as a "canary in the mine" for the coming depression, it is of little consequence to policy makers. Utility companies – like those supplying electricity and gas – are different because they operate and depend upon monopoly infrastructure. That is, while we can choose between supply companies for electricity, telephones and railway journeys, the customers of all of the companies use just the one network of electricity cables, telephone wires and mobile towers, and railway tracks. So that, when these supply companies fail through a loss of consumer demand, they present a risk to the network as a whole. Either the remaining companies have to take up the slack or government has – one way or another – to step in and bailout the system.

Another way of thinking about this is that private companies like *Wilco* are "discretionary." Sure, for some consumers, they can be an important source of discount supplies like household cleaning products. But when they close, customers can go elsewhere to buy the same products at more or less the same price. Utility companies – or at least some of them – are "essential," to our modern way of life. In the event, for example, that the water and sewage companies failed, we would face a wave of dehydration and disease which would put the recent Covid panic in its proper place as a relatively minor outbreak. Similarly, a loss of access to electricity and gas during winter would return us to conditions in which older and disabled people die much earlier from hypothermia or from cold-related illnesses.

In a *growing* economy this is of little concern, because consumers, businesses, and governments have the ability to fund the maintenance and expansion of the utilities while having sufficient excess demand to support a profitable discretionary economy. To most people, this is taken to mean an economy within which the money supply is expanding. But, as we have seen, the supply of currency can only expand in a benign way so long as there is sufficient untapped energy to absorb it. If not, surplus currency results in monetary inflation, in which any new currency serves only to devalue the currency already in circulation.

This is why the peak production of primary energy is so dangerous... and why the crisis first manifests in the economic sphere. Not only do we not have the surplus energy to continue to grow the economy, but since 2019 the energy available to us has been shrinking in two ways. First, and most obvious, total global "oil" production – in the broadest sense of the word – is still below its 2019 level, albeit significantly higher than the 2020 lockdown level. Second, and less obviously, the only production growth has been in "condensates" – the natural gas liquids which are too light to be refined into fuels... at least at an affordable cost. And since nothing happens in the economy without the energy to power it, the global economy *must* shrink accordingly.

Understanding this helps explain both why the USA and its European vassals rushed headlong into an economic war with Russia in the hope of destabilising the Putin government, balkanising the country, and thereby taking control of the country's fossil fuel and mineral resources. It also explains why – and only partly in response to this – some 75 percent of the world's states are actively working with the BRICS countries to develop an alternative, resource-based global trading and financial system. Moreover, and irrespective of what happens in Ukraine, the fact that the west clearly lost the economic war when sanctions backfired, means that the worst of the economic contraction is going to be experienced in the western states, with the developed economies of Europe facing the greatest decline.

The USA, which still has domestic reserves of fossil fuels and mineral resources is at least partially insulated from the inevitable blowback. The same cannot be said for the older European economies, whose rapid industrialisation in the nineteenth century exhausted their energy and mineral resources – a process that helped drive the imperialism that sought to carve up resource rich regions of Africa, Asia and South America by the beginning of the twentieth century. Those sources of energy and resources, of course, have long since been decolonised, so that access to western currencies was the only means by which Europe could continue to secure them. Which, again, is why locking down economies and thereby breaking global supply chains was a really bad idea, and why confiscating (i.e., stealing) the financial assets of Russian oligarchs has undermined the value of western banking and financial networks for non-western investors.

This raises a question which may be about to be answered in the most practical way... can a sovereign state go bankrupt? Technically, any state which issues its own currency cannot go bankrupt because it can simply print the currency needed to repay its debts. Schools of thought which promote this theory, however, tend to make the fundamental error of treating national economies as self-contained and self-standing. In practice, very few national economies have ever operated in isolation. And throughout history, relatively complex systems of international trade have been the norm. In the modern world, powered by vast quantities of fossil fuels, complexity and trade have been taken to undreamed of highs. So much so that – as we glimpsed during lockdown – any disruption threatens to undermine the system as a whole.

International finance – the so-called "Eurodollar system" (named for where it originated, not for where it operates) – has developed a global web of computerised exchanges for allowing trade to operate seamlessly. Go to a supermarket in Swindon in mid-winter, and you can purchase strawberries which had been picked on a farm outside Santiago just hours before. If you thought that the logistics of that operation – getting the pickers to the farm, getting the strawberries onto a truck, getting the truck to an airport, flying the plane from one side of the planet to the other, etc. – was mind boggling, imagine the systems which need to be in place to guarantee that the farmer, the pickers, the truck drivers, the aeroplane crew, and the supermarket workers can all get paid even before you arrived to swipe your debit card in exchange for those strawberries. And the same kind of process has to occur with every resource or good moved from one place to another across the global economy.

Spiriting currency out of thin air is the easy bit... thinking through what might happen to a government which did so is an altogether trickier matter. Consider the United Kingdom – a state which imports the majority of food, energy, resources, and goods that it consumes. It is also a state whose export statistics are flattering because most of what it does is to assemble components imported from elsewhere in the world. Its biggest *material* export is Scotch whisky – enjoyable but hardly essential – and its main source of international currency (mainly US dollars) is via the "export" of banking and financial services (i.e., *debt*). At the time of writing, it also happens to be a state whose public debt is 100 percent of its GDP.

So, could the UK simply spirit new pounds out of thin air to pay down at least some of its public debt? Sure, it *could* do that... in the same way that Weimar Germany printed Marks to repay reparations to France, or in the way Zimbabwe attempted to print its way to prosperity in the 1990s. Whether it would be *wise* to do anything like this is debateable, since the ensuing devaluation of the currency would result in massive import inflation which, in a country which imports 60 percent of its calories, 10 percent of its oil, and 20 percent of its electricity, would be devastating to living standards.

The problem is compounded in the UK because of a legacy culture of industrial abundance. In part, this stems from Britain being the first country to industrialise on the back of its vast coal reserves. This provided the basis for a British Empire which at its height covered a quarter of the world's habitable land mass. More recently though, it was the use of North Sea oil to obscure the UK's ongoing economic decline – and to underwrite the City of London banking and finance sector – which produced a psychology of invulnerability. What Britain might have been if those oil revenues had been invested back into its industrial base or if, like Norway and Saudi Arabia, a portion had been placed in a sovereign wealth fund, is moot. Because what the Thatcher government actually did was to squander it on unproductive tax cuts and papering over the negative impacts of economic decay. In this respect, Britain since the 1980s is merely a more complex version of every other oil state on the planet. As Leif Wenar[32] explains:

> "Oil wealth pours into these states, enriching elites, enabling corruption and repression, and damaging the prospects for economic development and good governance..."

Despite losing five million good industrial jobs – many of them due to oil overvaluing the UK's currency and making exports too expensive – in the recession of the early 1980s, living standards across the UK were higher than might have been expected. As Ian Jack[33] reminisced:

> "I had the idea... when I was walking through a London square around the time of the City's deregulatory 'Big Bang' and Peregrine Worsthorne coining the phrase 'bourgeois triumphalism' to describe the brash behaviour of the newly enriched: the boys who wore red braces and swore long and loud in restaurants. Champagne was becoming an unexceptional drink. The miners had been beaten. A little terraced house in an ordinary bit of London would buy 7.5 similar houses in Bradford. In the seven years since 1979, jobs in manufacturing had declined from about seven million to around five million, and more than nine in every 10 of all jobs lost were located north of the diagonal between the Bristol channel and the Wash. And yet it was also true that more people owned more things – tumble dryers and deep freezers – than ever before, and that the average household's disposable income in 1985 was more than 10% higher than it had been in the last days of Jim Callaghan's government.

> "Social peace had been bought by tax cuts and welfare benefits, and these had been largely enabled by government income from North Sea oil that by the mid-1980s was delivering the Treasury 10% of its revenues."

The Blair government was able to ride the oil boom, enjoying the illusory prosperity of a massive debt boom bought with the revenues from the North Sea. Indeed, in another "what if?" of British history, had it not been for the 1988 Piper Alpha disaster – which took out so much production that the UK had to import oil and gas again – there would have been no "Black Wednesday" in 1992, and John Major's government might have gone on to win the 1997 election. Nevertheless, Blair's good fortune was always going to be limited because North Sea production peaked in 1999, and had fallen by 60 percent by the 2005 election, leaving the UK increasingly dependent upon imported oil and gas, and leaving Britain poorly placed when the global debt bubble burst in 2008. As Euan Mearns[34] wrote a decade ago, the psychology of abundance persisted:

> "For decades the UK has been accustomed to filling its coffers with the bounty from North Sea oil and gas, and the jobs and tax receipts it has brought. At one time exports helped balance the books and provided energy security on our doorstep. But production peaked at the equivalent of 4.72 million barrels per day in 1999 and the subsequent decline has in recent years accelerated, as the figures from BP's statistical review of world energy 2013 show.

> "These days the UK is a net importer of oil and gas, and coal, accounting for £22 billion of the £59.8 billion deficit in the 2012 balance of payments."

It is hard to credit the 2010 Cameron government with any degree of foresight... they, after all, failed to foresee the outcome of an EU membership referendum which they assumed would be an easy win in 2016. Most likely, the austerity program they introduced from 2010 was driven by the instinctive Tory desire to kick the poor (Cameron had been a member of the Bullingdon Club, among who's many antisocial activities, was burning £50 notes in front of homeless people). However, were it not for measures designed to curb public spending, the UK would be in an even more difficult position than it is. This is because we are reaching public spending limits which will force us to test the proposition that a sovereign state can simply print the currency it needs... Britain may be among the first to have no alternative.

A year ago, under the disastrous – but fortunately brief – Liz Truss premiership, the UK faced the first rumblings of a sovereign debt crisis, when a package of ill-advised and uncosted tax cuts resulted in a crisis of confidence in the bond markets. Put simply, international investors refused to believe that Britain would be able to repay (the value of) its debts if the tax cuts went ahead. A quick intervention by the Bank of England, and the rapid ditching of Truss, calmed the markets. But the problem hasn't gone away.

A year later, the same issue manifested in a different way. Birmingham City Council – the biggest local administration in Europe – issued a so-called "Section 114 notice." This is the nearest a local government body can become to bankruptcy, because central government, one way or another, would have to maintain essential services, and central government cannot *technically* go bankrupt. One consequence – largely unseen by establishment journalists – was that international investors baulked at the prospect of government needing an unfunded bailout of Birmingham council – which would leave the UK government even less able to fund its borrowing. Moreover, Birmingham is far from the only UK council to have borrowed its way into de facto bankruptcy. Nor has any one party been particularly profligate. With less publicity, Tory-run Thurrock (£470m in debt) Labour-run Croydon (£1.6bn in debt) and Lib-Dem Woking (£2bn in debt) have all managed to rack up unsustainable debts which, collectively, may overwhelm an already indebted central government.

So long as the UK had its stream of oil and gas revenues to underwrite its borrowing, governments – local and central – could avoid difficult decisions, and simply make unfunded promises to the electorate, using low-interest debt to bridge the gap between income and expenditure. Indeed, even after the UK became a net importer of oil and gas, the globally low interest rates – especially after the 2008 crash – allowed the borrowing frenzy to continue. In the aftermath of lockdown, self-destructive sanctions, and the growth of an alternative trade bloc, import-inflation has risen, and UK interest rates have followed (UK "inflation" has been "stickier" than in neighbouring states).

It is the increased cost of debt-servicing which has caused the headline problem for local and central governments, which are paying an ever-higher proportion of their income to cover interest payments. But the deeper crisis will be maintaining tax income as private borrowing is hit by the new high interest conditions.

Interest rates are an incredibly blunt tool for addressing *monetary* inflation and have little impact at all on imported inflation. However, since they are the only tool in the central bank armoury, they have been applied in a cack-handed manner. If, as they often claim, the economists at the Bank of England knew what interest rate was required to bring down inflation, they would surely have set it at that rate. The fact that they have raised rates in small increments for the past two years suggests that they are clueless and are simply raising rates until something breaks and forces them to lower rates again. To some extent they can be forgiven, because the government has been asleep at the wheel – not only failing to take action to hold down prices, but actively engaging in stunts (like contributing £36bn to everyone's energy bills last winter) which have held prices up. Nevertheless, the big problem with interest rate rises is they can take months and years to have an effect. For example, some two million mortgages were taken out either side of the first lockdown, when interest rates were at a historic low. The first of these – taken out at a rate of two percent or more – have already fallen due and have already resulted in tens of thousands of households falling into arrears. But it is what is coming which is beginning to raise alarm bells. According to the UK's Office for National Statistics, 1.4 million low-interest mortgages will be rolled-over in the final quarter of 2023 and the first half of 2024. This will involve households which had been paying interest at 1.5 percent having to meet a new rate around 6.5 percent. And so, a family which bought a £250,000 house in 2020, and was repaying £906 a month, will now face a monthly payment of £1,864 if they can get a new fixed rate deal – if they go onto the standard variable rate, their payment will rise to £2,014... more than a thousand pounds per month more than they had been paying.

Even the highest earning households are unlikely to have – or be able to find – a spare £1,000 per month to bridge this gap. And most households are simply going to default. The banks will no doubt be the immediate casualty of this, since bad mortgages, most likely accompanied by bad business debt, will turn bank assets into liabilities – repossessing houses and businesses is expensive, takes time, and is unlikely to recover much value as both will be in negative equity. But whereas last time around governments could treat banks – and the financial sector more broadly – as too big to fail, this time around they are likely to be too big to *save*.

The UK illustrates this problem more clearly than elsewhere because it has become something of a basket case since the 1980s:

- Oil revenues covered the collapse of its economic base
- The projected taxes on oil allowed excess government borrowing
- As the oil goes away and the state is obliged to fall back on business and household taxes, its ability to continue borrowing is challenged
- As interest rates increase, its ability to service its dollar-denominated debt is impacted
- Faced with financial crises (local councils, mortgage defaults, business failures) government is less able to engage in bailouts
- Neither alternative option – raising interest rates to attract investors or creating currency to repay debts – can solve the problem because both drive up costs and exacerbate the crisis.

Less import-dependent states might survive for longer, along with those states whose energy consumption remains lower than their energy production. But even goods exporting states like Germany face serious disruption as the cost of both imported and domestic energy rises remorselessly. Indeed, the situation facing exporting states – including the world's biggest, China – looks a lot like Karl Marx's crisis of overproduction. Only the deepening indebtedness of importing states like the UK and the USA have allowed economies like China and Germany to maintain export *growth*. But now that the importing states are reaching limits, unsold inventories are building up, and new orders are falling. As a result, goods are piling up on Chinese docksides and warehouses, and factories are forced to slow down. As wages fall, so China's property Ponzi scheme faces collapse, taking its domestic economy with it.

Where China differs from Germany though, is that the Chinese leadership is far more aware of the importance of energy. From 2002, when it was admitted to the World Trade Organisation, China deliberately developed its manufacturing economy on the back of coal-power that the rest of the world was trying to turn its back on. Where Germany's leaders were talking about a "green" *Energiewende*, China was expanding its domestic coal production even as it ramped up imports of coal made cheap by western green policies. Today, China is also the biggest importer of Saudi Arabian and Iranian oil and is actively working with Russia to build pipelines to move Siberian oil and gas to China rather than to Europe. Indeed, even the development of electric cars and scooters in China owes more to the need to conserve oil for industrial use (effectively powering small vehicles with coal rather than petrol) than to any concern for the environment. And it is for this reason that China and its BRICS partners are set to be the last economies standing, while Germany and its European neighbours are on a fast-track to collapse.

Chapter 9

False Futures

Our tendency to attribute progress solely to the combination of human ingenuity and technology, remains one of our more suicidal flaws. Even though at face value, it seems so obvious that few even stop to think about it. If, by "progress," we mean more people living longer and at a higher standard of living, then both ingenuity and technology are intimately bound up in it. And since – *apparently* – the only limit to technology and ingenuity is our imagination, then there can be no limit to progress.

Take a look around you, however, and you might notice that progress has stalled. Life expectancy in the developed states has gone into reverse alongside birth rates... pointing to a real near-term population collapse. Standards of living for the majority, meanwhile, when adjusted for inflation, stalled in the 1970s and have been falling since at least 2008. At the same time, the technologies that were meant to propel humanity to the stars – space flight, supersonic commercial flight, etc. – ceased improving in the mid-1970s. Far more people remember Neil Armstrong and Buzz Aldrin than know who Gene Cernan was. When Armstrong and Aldrin set foot on the Moon on 20 July 1969, people around the world imagined this was the beginning of an Age of Discovery similar to, but far greater than the European discovery and colonisation of the Americas. But when, just three-and-a-half years later (14 December 1972) Cernan left the Lunar surface, humanity's journey beyond the near-Earth orbits of space stations (just a tenth of the distance to the Moon) was over. The new economic conditions – which were accelerated by the peak of US oil production and Nixon's decision to take the dollar off the gold standard – meant that the cost of manned space flight far exceeded any benefits.

Something similar happened to supersonic commercial flight. Around the time that Kennedy announced the plan to land men on the Moon – as much a Cold War contest as a scientific endeavour – French and British aviation engineers were planning the development of the world's first *commercial* supersonic aeroplane. Between 1963 and 1972, 18 companies had placed orders for 66 *Concordes*. But by the time *Concorde* made its first scheduled flight in January 1976, the excessive cost of the aeroplane in the stagflationary economy of the day had led to 46 of the orders being cancelled, with a further four being cancelled by 1980. In the end it was only the heavily-subsidised state airlines of Britain and France which ever operated *Concordes*... and only then at a loss. On 10 April 2003, following the Dotcom crisis in 2000, both airlines brought the era of commercial supersonic flight to an end. Passenger numbers had dropped even as operating costs had spiralled upward. In the end, it was more profitable to run fuel-efficient subsonic aeroplanes, even if journey times were longer.

At no stage in this process did we somehow forget how to do space travel or supersonic flight. Indeed, *unmanned* space travel has continued – although plutonium shortages threaten future long-range satellite missions. And, of course, military aircraft reach supersonic speeds day-in day-out. But surely, if human ingenuity and technology are all that is required for progress, the first Martian colonies ought to have been landed decades ago, while the rest of us ought to be whizzing across the world's oceans and continents faster than a speeding bullet. But we are not.

In a less high-profile example of technological reversal, at least in the UK, consider the disappearance of the once ubiquitous automated car wash. It used to be that these could be found at every filling station and supermarket in the country. But those which remain today are mostly a loss-leading service provided by big supermarkets – which hope to recoup the cost from sales within their stores. Rather like *Concorde* and *Apollo*, the operating and maintenance costs began to spiral even as the profit margins of the operators were squeezed. So that, rather than maintain them, many operators simply demolished them once parts needed to be replaced. And insofar as British drivers still pay to have their cars washed, it will usually be at a labour-intensive hand car wash – all too often provided by migrant workers paid below the minimum wage.

In another example just prior to the Pandemic, something odd happened in the world of motorcycling. After decades of technological improvement and enhancement, an Indian company with a British name – Royal Enfield – took the world's best seller slot with the 650cc *Interceptor* – a machine which abandoned all but the legal technological requirements such as anti-lock braking. Where other motorcycle companies were still asking for thousands of pounds extra for stereo, satnav, keyless ignition, hand warmers, ipod docks, etc., Royal Enfield kept it simple and benefited from a post-2008 consumer base which proved happy to put cost ahead of luxury.

Pointing out that there is *something* about cost versus benefits which can negate human ingenuity and technology sounds mean. And, sure, when it is stated in purely monetary terms, it is easy to dismiss as such, since the wealth nominally held by the global billionaire class is surely great enough to fund any technological endeavour if only we had the political will. This though, is an illusion, as it begs the question of how we might *liquidate* that hypothetical wealth. The financial dimension of the problem is simply that there is nobody with sufficient cash to by the nominal assets – shares, bonds, property, precious metals, etc. – nominally held by the billionaire class. Nor could members of the billionaire class sell their assets for cash without hugely devaluing them. Only governments – with their sovereign privilege of being able to print currency out of thin air – could find the necessary cash. But if cash was the only issue, why use it to buy assets at all? Why not just create new currency to directly resurrect manned space flight, supersonic passenger flights, hi-tech motorcycles, automated car washes, and everything in between?

This brings us to the *thermodynamic* dimension of the problem. If finance were the sole problem facing us, we might easily have central banks conjure into existence new supersonic airliners, rockets to the Moon, and enough wind turbines and solar panels to reverse global warming. But as we have seen, money is merely a claim on goods, services and resources in the real world. And – as we are currently witnessing – in the event that governments and central banks are foolish enough to create additional currency when the economy does not have access to the additional goods, services and resources to match, we get *inflation*.

The problem goes deeper though, because there are plenty of under-employed people who could produce goods and services to match the new currency. But they haven't. And this suggests that the problem goes back to the resources needed to manufacture the goods and to operate the services. However, there is an almost infinite supply of resources on planet Earth, *if only we had the means to harvest them*. If, for example, we could create giant pumps and filters to hoover up millions of gallons of sea water, we could recover undreamed of quantities of all of the mineral resources required to continue growing the global economy... but, of course, we can't.

This brings us to the root of the problem – *energy*. The thing which is lacking from our theoretical ability to land people on the Moon, to fly around the world faster than the speed of a bullet, to generate hundreds of thousands of terawatts of electricity from wind and sunlight, or to filter rare minerals from sea water is the absence of the *surplus* energy required to make it happen... and even here, not all energy is equal.

Electricity is great at powering the global communications system, Bank computers, data centres, computers, smartphones, and GPS systems. But it is an inefficient way of powering vehicles – and cannot power long-haul trucks, industrial and agricultural machinery, long-distance shipping or all but the smallest aeroplanes and shortest flights. With one exception – photovoltaic panels – all electricity is generated in the same way – by spinning copper coils around a magnet. The most efficient way of doing this is with nuclear power, which uses the same turbines as coal, but which produces thousands of times the heat per unit of fuel. But both coal and nuclear suffer from being too unresponsive to fluctuations in demand. Which is why electricity generators in the developed states moved to a combination of nuclear (for baseload) and gas (for rapidly increasing and decreasing supply to meet demand). Indeed, by using this combination, France is far and away the biggest generator of zero-carbon electricity in Europe... despite the German and UK government claims to being the "greenest."

Where France has maintained and extended its nuclear generation, Germany – for insane reasons – and the UK – for short-term political gain – have allowed nuclear power to be phased out. As a result, both turned to wind turbines to fill a gap which they are ill-fitted for at that scale. Wind turbines suffer the opposite problem to coal and nuclear – supply varies second-to-second according to what the wind is doing. And since – at least for now – the grid operators have no means of controlling second-to-second demand, both Germany and the UK turned to gas to plug the gap. And so long as the European wholesale market for gas was awash with cheap supplies from Russia, the North Sea and Qatar, there seemed to be no limit to the amount of wind capacity which could be deployed.

The problem with "green" energy though, doesn't end with balancing moment-to-moment supply and demand. There is also the thorny issue of energy storage. The big advantage of fossil fuels and nuclear is that the fuels *are* the energy store, so that all the operators need to do is to increase the fission, turn up the gas, or throw some more coal into the furnace. But we cannot throw additional wind at a windfarm when the wind isn't blowing. Which is a particular problem in Germany and the UK, where winter high pressure weather systems can cause weeks of low wind at precisely the time when people need the additional power. Even at today's concentrations, the UK has to operate a scheme for heavy industry to close down during periods of low wind. And more recently, it has begun paying high-consuming households to curb their consumption during low wind periods.

The media/activist (non) solution is battery technology – which is wrongly treated as a novel technology to which the holy mantra of Big Tech may be applied:

- It is only a prototype
- It will improve
- It is inevitable.

But battery technology – like wind turbines themselves – has been around for decades, so that all of the cheap and easy productivity gains (and most of the expensive and difficult) have already been achieved. So that the best we can manage – the $600 million Moss Landing Energy Storage Facility in Monterey County, California is to store and then provide enough backup electricity to power a large city for around an hour. For around the same price (£425 million) the Dinorwig pumped hydro station in North Wales can supply the same large city for a little over 12 hours. The problem with pumped hydro being that there are only so many unpopulated valleys that can be dammed and high mountains that can be hollowed out.

This is "green" electricity's first dirty secret. Whichever way you approach the problem, you have to turn to fossil fuels – primarily gas – to plug the baseload and intermittency gaps. But the supposed "energy transition" has an even dirtier secret... a form of out-of-sight/out-of-mind.

When politicians and activists set their *Energiewende*/net zero targets, they saw the project in financial terms. How many wind turbines, solar panels and batteries do we need, multiplied by the cost (at the time of planning) of constructing and deploying them. It was then just a matter of governments providing subsidies while encouraging private capital to invest – carbon credits and ESG (environment, social and governance) rating helping to drive the necessary investment. But none of the material inputs cost what they cost.

Take lithium carbonate – the base mineral for producing batteries – at the beginning of the century, the price was less than $2,000 per tonne. By 2010, with demand rising, this had risen to $5,180 per tonne and reaching what was believed to be a high point of $16,000 per tonne in 2018, before demand fell in the 2019 recession and the two years of lockdown which followed (Fig 18).

Average lithium carbonate price 2010-2022

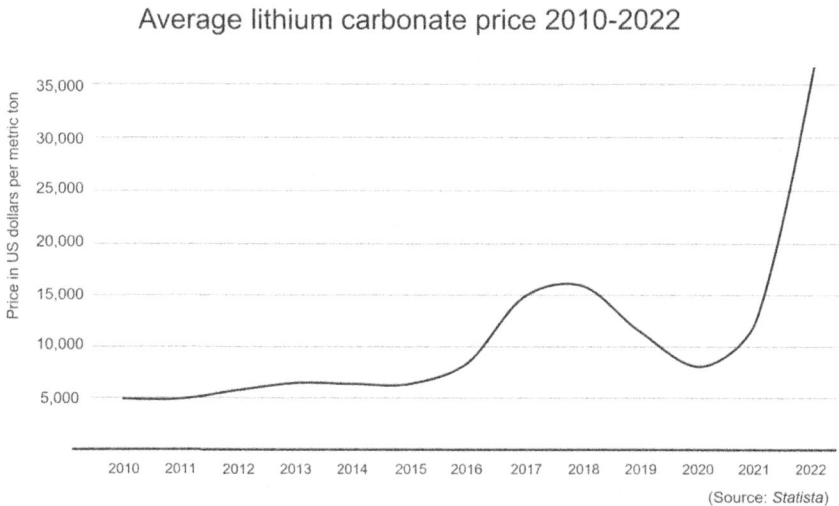

(Source: *Statista*)

Figure 18: Lithium is only cheap if demand is low and energy is cheap

Having reached $53,000 per tonne in the first quarter of 2023, the price has fallen to $22,800 today, reflecting the big downturn in China, which consumes more than half of the world's lithium production.

Nor is this solely due to exploding demand and access to cheap credit. The cost of energy also plays a large part in the cost of manufacturing, deploying, and maintaining wind turbines and solar panels. Europe's wind turbine manufacturing, for example, used to be located primarily in Germany, where access to cheap Russian fossil fuels and mineral resources kept costs to a minimum. But following the ill-advised decision to eschew further imports of cheap fossil fuels in response to Russia's invasion of Ukraine, the first casualties were the smelting plants and steelworks which provided the raw materials, followed by the wind turbine plants themselves. Other states, like the UK, whose net zero targets assumed ongoing access to relatively cheap German-made wind turbines, are now having to look to China and the USA to supply them at a much higher cost.

The impact of the disruption in renewable energy-harvesting technologies is also seen in the financial sector, where shares in the sector have crashed. As George Steer at the *Financial Times*[35] reports:

"The S&P Global Clean Energy Index, which is made up of 100 of the biggest companies in solar, wind power and other renewables-related businesses, has dropped 20.2 per cent over the past two months.

"That has put it on course for its worst annual performance since 2013. By contrast, the oil and gas-heavy S&P 500 Energy Index has added 6 per cent...

"The decline comes despite tens of billions of dollars in tax credits, subsidies and loans being offered by governments to green energy companies in the US and Europe.

"The renewable sector has been particularly vulnerable to rising interest rates because many companies agree long-term contracts, fixing the price at which they will sell energy, before developing their projects."

A similar crisis occurred in the UK, where an auction of licences to supply wind energy to the Grid, based on where prices were expected to be if pre-2020 trends had continued, attracted no bidders. Rising energy, labour and raw material costs blew out of the water[36] the claim that renewable energy would continue to get cheaper – exposing the reality that, like everything else in the economy, the cost (although not always the price) rises and falls in line with the cost of primary energy... oil.

This would seem to nullify any claim that humanity can maintain its advanced economies *and* raise the living standards of the rest of the world using non-renewable renewable energy-harvesting technologies (NRREHTs) alone. But the sheer scale of the endeavour – replacing the annual 137,236.67 Terawatt hours of energy we consume from oil, coal and gas, with wind and solar which currently accounts for just 6.5 percent (8,935.84 Terawatt hours) of that – raises questions about whether there is anywhere near enough of Planet Earth to provide the resources (Fig 19).

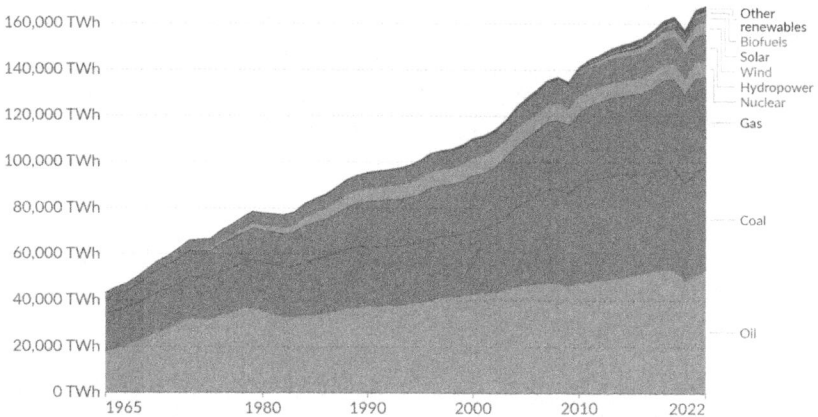

Energy consumption by source, World

Primary energy consumption is measured in terawatt-hours (TWh). Here an inefficiency factor (the 'substitution' method) has been applied for fossil fuels, meaning the shares by each energy source give a better approximation of final energy consumption.

Source: Energy Institute Statistical Review of World Energy (2023)   OurWorldInData.org/energy • CC BY
Note: 'Other renewables' includes geothermal, biomass and waste energy.

Figure 19: NRREHTs Are a small fraction of a global energy mix which keeps growing

Presented with what has been proposed by the politicians who mendaciously call themselves "leaders," it is clear that we will not be reaching net zero in anything like the manner we have been promised. As Roger Pielke explained in a *Forbes* article[37] in 2019:

"In 2018 the world consumed 11,743 mtoe [mega tonnes of oil equivalent] in the form of coal, natural gas and petroleum. The combustion of these fossil fuels resulted in 33.7 billion tonnes of carbon dioxide emissions. In order for those emissions to reach net-zero, we will have to replace about 12,000 mtoe of energy consumption expected for 2019...

"To achieve net-zero carbon dioxide emissions globally by 2050 thus requires the deployment of >1 mtoe of carbon-free energy consumption (12,000 mtoe/11,051 days) every day, starting tomorrow and continuing for the next 30+ years. Achieving net-zero also requires the corresponding equivalent decommissioning of more than 1 mtoe of energy consumption from fossil fuels every single day...

"So the math here is simple: to achieve net-zero carbon dioxide emissions by 2050, the world would need to deploy 3 Turkey Point nuclear plants worth of carbon-free energy every two days, starting tomorrow and continuing to 2050. At the same time, a Turkey Point nuclear plant worth of fossil fuels would need to be decommissioned every day, starting tomorrow and continuing to 2050.

"I've found that some people don't like the use of a nuclear power plant as a measuring stick. So we can substitute wind energy as a measuring stick. Net-zero carbon dioxide by 2050 would require the deployment of 1500 wind turbines (2.5 MW) over 300 square miles, every day starting tomorrow and continuing to 2050..."

Even if we were to provide a realistic time frame – perhaps aiming to achieve the transition by 2250 rather than 2050 – serious doubts have been raised about the availability of the minerals required. After all, as Kurt Cobb[38] explains:

"The International Energy Agency (IEA) has attempted to project the needs of this new economy. The IEA's report entitled "The Role of Critical Minerals in Clean Energy Transitions" contains some eye-popping statistics that drive home just how much in the way of metals might be needed in order to supply the builders of this clean energy infrastructure.

"Using two scenarios the IEA estimated that growth in demand coming from clean energy industries just for battery-related minerals will explode by 2040 relative to 2020:

1. Lithium: Between 13 to 42 times.
2. Graphite: Between 8 and 25 times.
3. Cobalt: Between 6 to 21 times.
4. Nickel: Between 6 to 19 times.
5. Manganese: Between 3 to 8 times.

"Demand related specifically to renewable energy and its infrastructure is projected to increase for the following minerals under two scenarios:

1. Rare earth elements (REEs): Between 3.4 and 7.3 times more. REEs are important for electric motors and generators.
2. Molybdenum: Between 2.2 to 2.9 times more. Molybdenum is used in solar and wind power because of its ability to transmit electricity well.
3. Copper - Between 1.7 to 2.7 times more. Copper, of course, has long been used in electrical motors and wires.
4. Silicon - Between 1.8 to 2.3...

"What is not often discussed is the vast number of new mines which will have to be discovered, developed and operated in the coming years. It is not certain enough deposits of sufficient concentration to justify mine development will be found to supply these huge new sources of demand.

"And when economically viable deposits are found, their development and operation will consume a large amount of liquid fuels. Currently, almost all of those fuels are derived from oil and to a much smaller extent natural gas. This mine build-out will result in significant ongoing emissions of greenhouse gases. And the refining of these metals will require copious amount of energy to achieve the high temperatures required..."

Professor Simon Michaux from the Geological Survey of Finland goes much further in setting out the likely resource implications of a transition from fossil fuels to a combination of renewable and nuclear energy. In a 1,000-page technical assessment[39], Michaux calculates the energy mix required to phase out fossil fuels, and the resource implications that this will have:

"A novel bottom-up approach (as opposed to the typical top-down approach) was used to make the calculations presented here. Previous studies have also tended to focus on estimated costs of production and CO_2 footprint metrics, whereas the present report is based on the physical material requirements...

"Calculations reported here suggest that the total additional non-fossil fuel electrical power annual capacity to be added to the global grid will need to be around 37,670.6 TWh. If the same non-fossil fuel energy mix as that reported in 2018 is assumed, then this translates into an extra 221,594 new power plants will be needed to be constructed and commissioned. To put this in context, the total power plant fleet in 2018 (all types including fossil fuel plants) was only 46,423 stations. This large number reflects the lower Energy Returned on Energy Invested (ERoEI) ratio of renewable power compared to current fossil fuels."

Remember that the stated aim is to achieve this by 2050, and yet, what is proposed is the consumption of centuries' – and in some cases millennia's – worth of some mineral resources at current rates of production (Fig 20).

Metal	Element	Total metal required produce one generation of technology units to phase out fossil fuels (tonnes)	Global Metal Production 2019 (tonnes)	Years to produce metal at 2019 rates of production (years)
Copper	Cu	4 575 523 674	24 200 000	189,1
Nickel	Ni	940 578 114	2 350 142	400,2
Lithium	Li	944 150 293	95 170 *	9920,7
Cobalt	Co	218 396 990	126 019	1733,0
Graphite (natural flake)	C	8 973 640 257	1 156 300 ♦	3287,9
Graphite (synthetic)	C		1 573 000 ♦	-
Silicon (Metallurgical)	Si	49 571 460	8 410 000	5,9
Vanadium	V	681 865 986	96 021 *	7101,2
Rare Earth Metals	-			
Neodymium	Nd	965 183	23 900	40,4
Germanium	Ge	4 163 162	143	29113,0
Lanthanum	La	5 970 738	35 800	166,8
Praseodymium	Pr	235 387	7 500	31,4
Dysprosium	Dy	196 207	1 000	196,2
Terbium	Tb	16 771	280	59,9

* Estimated from mining production. All other values are refining production values.

♦ Natural flake graphite and synthetic graphite was combined to estimate total production

(Source: BGR 2021, USGS, Friedrichs 2022)

Figure 20: the eye-watering mineral demands of a NRREHTs transition

Remember too, that humans already know what a "green" economy looks like... it is what humans have been doing for all but the last 300 out of the last 200,000 or so years. Indeed, the Anglo-Saxon economy of England during the five centuries between the fall of the Western Roman Empire and the arrival of the Normans was among the most "sustainable" of all. We know this because almost nothing of that economy survives in the archaeological record beyond post holes and a few shards of low-quality pottery.

In this sense, returning to some kind of "green" economy is simple enough (although getting from here to there is likely to be chaotic and homicidal). Having anything like the current standards of living, even in the developing world, without fossil fuels, on the other hand, is simply impossible. And anyone claiming such a transition can be achieved in just three decades – at least without some hugely powerful new energy source – is clearly in urgent need of a place in an insane asylum.

This though, disguises the true predicament that humanity finds itself in. Because moving away from fossil fuels – remembering that the energy cost of all three is determined by the energy cost of oil – is *not a choice*, but a thermodynamic fact:

- The size of untapped oil reserves is falling,
- The difficulty of recovering reserves is increasing,
- The nature of the remaining oil is changing – less conventional crude, more condensates and bitumen,
- The thermal content of the remaining oil is lower,
- Oil- producing states are holding onto a greater share of the reserves to power their domestic economies – raising prices and creating shortages in oil-consuming states,
- The energy cost of recovering and consuming oil is increasing, causing the *surplus* energy to power the economy to decline.

The question is not *if* the economy is going to shrink, but whether there is a way of managing decline without some kind of catastrophic collapse into barbarism or life-ending war as people scramble for the remaining resources.

Chapter 10

This time *really* is different

Energy shocks of the kind set out here are nothing new. One of the reasons for the collapse of the Western Roman Empire is that they chopped down too many of their trees – which at the time were used both as a construction material and a fuel. In sixteenth century Europe, timber shortages were also commonplace – one reason why the forested English and French colonies of North America proved to be wealthier in the long-term than the gold and silver rich Central and South American colonies of Spain and Portugal. Elsewhere, shortages of food – the earliest energy source of all – could bring ruin to previously prosperous economies. The changing climate in fourteenth century Europe led to poorer harvests which, in turn weakened the population, making it more vulnerable to the arrival of the plague in the 1340s. It is also now thought that the collapse of the first world economy around 1186 BCE began with a similar shift in climate causing poorer harvests and weakening the population. The arrival of the "sea people" most likely marking the end of a period of decline rather than its cause.

Nevertheless, since all pre-industrial economies had to get by on the annual solar energy available to them, for most ordinary people the difference between a growing and a declining economy was relatively small. Far smaller, for example, than the gulf in the experience of a semi-skilled western worker in 1960 and his or her counterpart today. In 1960, the wage of a semi-skilled worker would allow him to buy a house, raise a family, run a car, and pay for an annual holiday. In 2023, the wage of a semi-skilled worker is barely sufficient to keep him off the street – owning a house, raising a family, buying a car and taking a holiday are these days luxuries that only those in a dwindling managerial class can take for granted.

This said, insofar as today's semi-skilled worker might afford the rent on a small bedsit, with enough left over to buy a reasonable diet and to operate a heater in winter, he might still be looked upon with a degree of envy by his Victorian counterpart, whose pay might cover the cost of a rope to hang across during the night, whose heating might be no more than old newsprint stuffed beneath his jacket, and whose access to fresh food would be limited. And while today's semi-skilled worker might fall back on publicly funded health and social security, with the small respite of a pension at the end of his life, his Victorian counterpart had no safety net beyond an early death in the Workhouse.

Historians and economists struggle to explain these differences because, with a few notable exceptions, they are "energy-blind." Prior to the 1980s, it had been possible to appeal to a kind of social enlightenment coupled to something called "progress." The belief being that following the European enlightenment and the ensuing industrial revolution, humanity was on an upward arc of progress in which *all* would be better off... eventually.

This would not necessarily have been obvious to the urban workers of the early industrial period, many of whom had been driven off the land by voracious landowners who could make more money raising sheep than they could from the rents of former peasants. Urban housing was cramped and insanitary, and industrial working conditions were toxic and often fatal. And it was only the impact of stunted child development on the military which began to drive reform.

At the same time, the Poor Law, which operated well within the rural village broke down with the anonymity of the new urban towns. In the pre-industrial poor law, the community – parish – was considered responsible for looking after its own. Of interest, there was no such thing as "old age" in chronological terms in this system. Pensions were given to those too *infirm* to work, which often corresponded with chronological old age, but old age alone was not a valid reason for drawing a pension. This, in turn, shaped the experience of poverty within the system – young, itinerant male workers being most at risk, and older women least so. This all changed with the reform of the Poor Law in the 1870s in response to urbanisation. Instead of holding the parish responsible for its people, the urban Poor Law placed responsibility on the family. Moreover, the conditions for receiving relief were stricter, with the threat of going into the workhouse being an ever-present danger (not least for young women, who were regularly abused as domestic labour for a new class of idle wives of the industrial rich, and frequently as unwilling sexual partners of the industrialists themselves). Perhaps the biggest victims of the urban Poor Law though, were the older women who, in the rural system had been looked after, but who, because of the poverty of their families – now ended their days in the squalor of the Workhouse.

Even as late as the inter-war years, the condition of the urban poor was the source of political and economic dispute. The wartime promise of "homes for heroes" remained unfilled. And while the worst excesses of the urban Poor Law had been tempered by the Liberal reforms from 1906, those on the wrong end of the deindustrialisation of the Great Depression were barely better off than their grandparents had been.

For ordinary working people, progress, then, was a very recent – and all too brief – phenomenon. Only following the reconstruction after the Second World War did real wages begin to rise. And, indeed, for the only time in history, the workers' share of the proceeds rose faster than the share taken by the ownership and investor classes. It is from this period too, that Margaret Thatcher developed her idea of a "home owning democracy" – because – at least for some workers – wages were rising faster than inflation, a large part of the *value* of a mortgage was inflated away by the time it ended. In effect, the banks were taking a big hit to the profits they could make on a mortgage. Unfortunately, the actions the Thatcher government was to take to cut inflation, effectively pulled the rug out from beneath her home owning democracy by creating today's conditions in which a growing tenant class cannot even get on the housing ladder but where social housing for rent has all but disappeared.

The retreat of prosperity from the 1970s, which led to the North-South divide of the 1980s, the archipelago of top-tier university districts of the early 2000s, and the handful of gated and security guarded housing developments of the post-lockdown economy, calls into question the very idea of progress. Certainly, the optimistic future of the BBC *Tomorrow's World* series failed to put in an appearance. Computerisation and miniaturisation proved an interesting distraction, but even these were unable to break the laws of physics. And so, we have had to forego our flying cars and holidays on the Moon. And let's not get into "energy too cheap to meter." For the bottom third of the population of the western economies in 2023, just staying warm and reasonably well fed has become a struggle.

Rather than the ever upward arc of progress, the spurt of exponential growth in the post-war years looks more like the left-hand side of a bell curve. The equal and opposite declining slope beginning sometime between 1980 and 2000 (Fig 21).

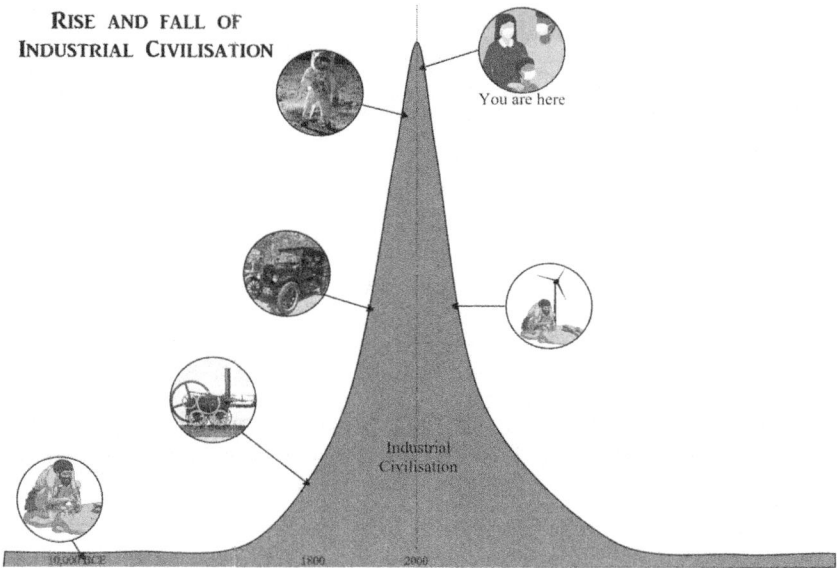

RISE AND FALL OF
INDUSTRIAL CIVILISATION

You are here

Industrial
Civilisation

10,900 BCE   1800   2000

Figure 21: the rise and fall of industrial civilisation

Those who pay little attention to the role of energy in the economy might object that the idea of the bell curve of progress has been around since Malthus. But at each turn, human ingenuity and technology have ridden to the rescue, ushering a new upward arc. And, of course, this is true so far as it goes. But the ingenuity and technology were always bound up with the primary energy of the period. Once the economy had begun to make the switch from charcoal to coal, it was only a matter of time before people began to use steam engines as an additional, and potentially more powerful, source of power. And once the basic steam technology had been developed, it would soon give rise to a series of productivity improvements which would pave the way for railways and steamships. Moreover, no longer tied to place in the way waterpower was, coal-fired steam power could provide the energy for manufacturing within the heart of the growing towns and cities, bringing down the cost of production and paving the way for further growth.

Productivity, however, follows an "S" curve rather than an ever upward arc. Once a technology has been developed, a series of cheap and easy improvements can usually be made. These, in turn, allow for greater profitability as the cost of inputs is lowered even as the volume of output is increased. But soon enough, we run out of cheap and easy improvements, leaving us with just the difficult and expensive... which means that further profitability is limited (Fig 22).

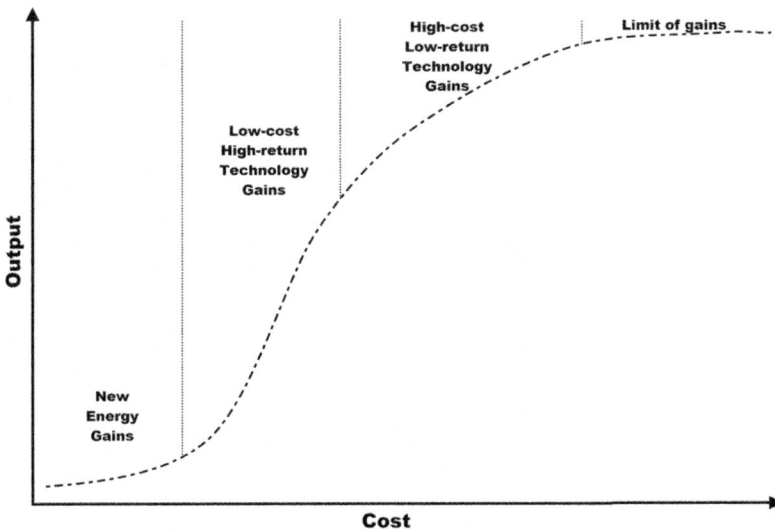

Figure 22: the productivity "S" curve

Although one might argue, for example, that the peak of steam powered locomotives only arrived with the Pacific Class in the 1930s, and with *Mallard* reaching the speed record of 126mph in July 1938, most of the cheap and easy productivity gains had been discovered a century before. And while the Pacific Class were a miracle of engineering, reducing to a minimum the amount of waste heat, they proved too expensive to operate and helped to bankrupt the British railways of the 1930s (slower electric trains would have been a better energy investment).

A similar process can be found with the development of aeroplanes, from the *Wright Flyer* to *Concorde* and, indeed, from the V2 rocket to the Saturn V which powered the Moon landings – although these are technologies of the oil age rather than the coal age. And that is the point so often overlooked by economists – the limits of the primary energy of an age set the upper limit of its economy (Fig 23).

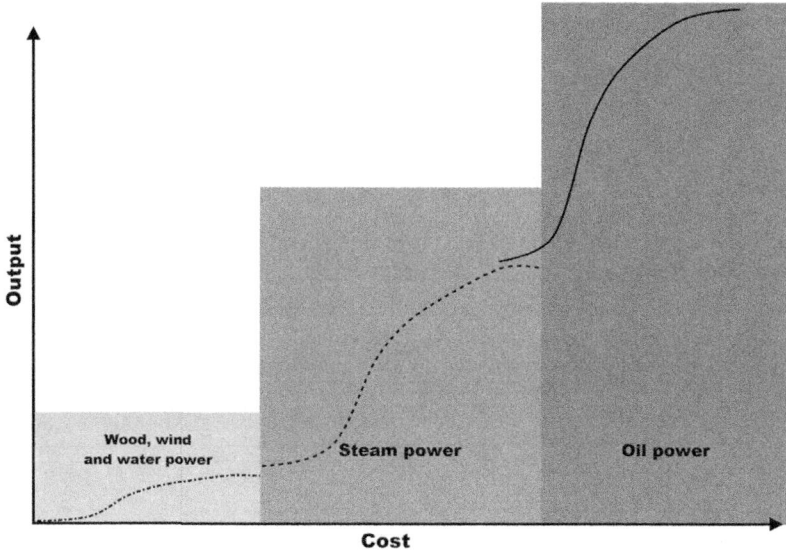

Figure 23: the three energy-productivity "S" curves of industrial civilisation

What humanity has lived through over the last three centuries is a combination of these productivity S-curves and the transition to a new, *energy-dense* and *more powerful* primary energy source. This explains the so-called "productivity puzzle" which exercises so many economists in the modern world. "Why is it," they ask, "that despite funnelling more and more money and expertise at the problem, further productivity fails to occur?" Well, now you know. It is because we have reached the limits to what is technically possible using oil age technologies.

Nor do the alternative energy sources on offer give any cause for comfort. Wind and solar – which are proposed more as a solution to carbon emissions than to economic growth – are too diffuse and too weak to provide even a small fraction of the power provided by oil. Which is why, for the most part, they have been used in an attempt to phase out coal (which more often means burning coal in China and India rather than not burning coal at all) while having little impact on oil. Hydro-electric and geothermal power is far greater than wind and solar but is geographically limited. And most of the best locations have already been developed. Nuclear – which a large part of the political and activist class continues to oppose out of a misinformed belief that they lead to nuclear weapons proliferation – is *slightly* different insofar as the energy-density of Uranium is vasty greater than that of the fossil fuels… in physics terms, the difference between the energy released by breaking the neutron bonds of an atom rather than the electron bonds. The problem with nuclear being that we have yet to figure out how to harness the potential energy – in a technically advanced manner. Nuclear power stations still use Victorian steam turbines to generate electricity. Furthermore, the cost of building these power stations all but rules out the likelihood of nuclear power replacing fossil fuels.

This time is different because, unlike every previous economic depression of the industrial age, there is no new, more energy-dense and versatile energy source waiting in the wings to provide the surplus energy to propel us into a new age of growth as magical to us as our own world would appear to a nineteenth century farmworker. Instead, we are witnessing the desperate *addition* of NRREHTs and nuclear power to an already declining fossil fuel store.

For the moment, we have reached a kind of plateau of energy production. Volumes of coal, gas and oil are holding up, although it is far from clear that production can be maintained at these levels for much longer. Nevertheless, because of the additional energy cost of maintaining this level of production, the amount of *surplus* energy available to power the wider, non-energy sectors of the economy is already falling fast. This, in turn, is why we have been living through a growing economic depression – punctuated by a series of worsening crashes – since the 1970s, and why we have now reached an economic point of no return.

Absolute energy shortages – in which no amount of money will be able to secure a supply – are some distance in the future. For the time being, "shortage" is manifesting in higher prices alongside falling living standards, so that a growing proportion of the population can no longer afford to consume energy at rates taken for granted just a couple of decades ago. At the bottom of the income ladder, people have all but ceased direct consumption of energy entirely – no longer owning a vehicle and shivering in the dark at home. Even the most basic energy source – food – is increasingly supplied by a massive network of foodbank charities to families which can no longer afford an adequate diet. Higher up the income ladder, all but the top 20 percent have been obliged to cut energy consumption – albeit in a far less traumatic fashion than those at the bottom. Cars are used less often for non-essential journeys, home heating is turned down, lighting and appliances are no longer left on, and even the nature of food shopping has changed with fewer luxury items and more value products being bought.

It is though, in the much larger economic arena of discretionary goods and services that the loss of surplus energy is becoming apparent. As the cost of essentials like food and fuel has increased, so consumption of everything else has been dramatically curtailed. Until recently, this could be hidden in the reporting of official retail statistics because although we – collectively – have been buying far less goods and services, a combination of lockdown handouts and credit card borrowing had allowed us to continue spending more month on month. But with the lockdown currency having returned to the circle of Hell from whence it was spirited by central bankers and government ministers, with our credit cards maxed-out, and with banks no longer prepared to extend credit which they no longer trust will be repaid, we have now entered a period in which both the volume and the value of our spending is in decline.

There will come a time when *absolute* energy shortages become apparent. Indeed, because of the deranged energy policies pursued in supposedly advanced states like Britain and Germany, the first shortages will likely be in an under-supply of electricity. In the UK, for example, all but three coal power stations have been demolished, and a large part of the nuclear fleet will close by 2025. The wind turbines and solar panels which were meant to fill the gap (leaving intermittency issues aside) did not get built, so that the UK now depends upon imports from Europe to plug a 20 percent hole in supply – that is the same Europe which can no longer meet its own electricity demand because its leaders decided that doing without essential supplies of Russian gas would be a good idea.

Gas shortages may well appear too, now that we have to rely upon liquified gas from Qatar and the USA to plug the gap. However, gas shortages are also likely to be experienced as electricity power cuts because gas grid operators fear the consequences of cutting the domestic supply. That is, if the domestic gas supply had to be cut, a national effort to make sure all gas appliances had been switched of would be required before a safe restart could be carried out – the risk being widespread gas explosions if gas leaked from appliances which had been left on.

Petroleum fuel shortages will likely take longer to appear, since rationing by price can continue for some time. However, as global supplies are diverted away from the UK and Europe, and with the USA unable to fully meet its domestic demand, some form of state intervention is coming sooner rather than later, if only to guarantee that critical transport needs are maintained. Moreover, public rationing, when it finally arrives, may not stop at limits on the amount of petrol someone can buy, but may also extend to public transport journeys too.

The economic spillover from these gathering energy shortages will likely involve a big increase in unemployment as whole swathes of the discretionary economy become insolvent. Things that we took for granted just a few years ago – holidays abroad, meals out at restaurants, high fashion, car ownership, etc., are likely to become luxuries affordable only to the rich (as they had been prior to the post-war boom). Although *exactly* how this plays out *politically* is anybody's guess. Certainly, the populist revolt in 2016, which led to the UK leaving the European Union and the election of Donald Trump in the USA was fuelled by discontent across those parts of the UK and US economies which have been stagnating since the depression of the 1980s. Not only has the populist wave not gone away, but – as successive elections across the EU have demonstrated – the appetite for change has grown even stronger. At the same time the established centre-left and centre-right parties seem neither to comprehend the gathering storm, still less offer feasible solutions – a recipe for the growth of extremist politics which will leave Trump and Farage looking like moderates in comparison.

Absent some yet-to-be-discovered new energy source though, no political program which promises a return to growth can succeed. The best we might do is to arrive at a consensus instead, over how to manage a process of decline. But there is no economic theory nor university economics department which even considers this a possibility. And for the moment, any politician who calls for managed de-growth is simply not going to be elected. And so, we are likely to be entering a period of denial and delusion as we reach for ever less plausible attempts to restore a high-energy economy in a low-energy environment.

Afterworld

It is at this point in all of the best-selling books, that I am meant to reveal the solution to our problems... the new energy sources and technologies which will rescue us at the end of the oil age in the same way that oil rescued people from the Great depression which followed the end of the coal age. I wish I could do so. But there is no magic energy source or new technology waiting just over the horizon to rescue us from what must otherwise be the downslope of the bell curve of industrial civilisation. Oil – a geologically limited and increasingly too expensive – fuel source is the best we could manage. And, as the limits both oil itself and the oil age technologies it allowed are reached, we have but two choices – learn to manage and live with a shrinking economy or turn to ever more outlandish non-solutions which promise – in quasi-religious fashion – to save us from the fate which awaits civilisations as surely as it awaits each of the individuals within them.

I am reminded of G.K. Chesterton's *Ballad of the White Horse*, where King Alfred (of burned scones fame) asks of the apparition of the White Lady what the outcome of the coming battle between his army and those of the Vikings will be. To which the White Lady replies:

I offer you naught for your comfort

Yea naught for your desire

Save that the sky grows darker yet

And the sea rises higher.

None of us can predict exactly how the future will unfold. Although we ought to at least agree that the future will still have to conform to the laws of physics. And since surplus energy sets a limit upon the size of the economy which no amount of currency creation or political posturing can change, then – absent an energy miracle – we are living through an inflection point between the growing economy of the industrial age and the shrinking economy of the post-industrial era... to repeat Soddy for a third time, "if only we had known it, it might have been a merrier age!"

Notes

1. Watkins, T. 2015. *The Consciousness of Sheep.* Waye Forward Publishing

2. Soddy, F. 1932. *Wealth and Debt: The solution of the economic paradox.* Britons Publishing Company.

3. Hubbert, M.K. 1956. *Nuclear Energy and Fossil Fuels.* Shell Development Company, Publication No. 95.

4. For as detailed calculation of the thermodynamic limits imposed by peak oil, see: Warm, B. 2023. *The Last Years of the Oil Age: Physics kills oil and cars.* www.researchgate.net/publication/369388244

5. Bank of England. 1 October 2019. *How is money created?* www.bankofengland.co.uk/explainers/how-is-money-created

6. Soddy, F. 1933. *Wealth and Debt: The Solution of the Economic Paradox* (currently out of print)

7. Solomon, G.S. 2014. *The living standards of Tyneside coal miners, 1836-1862.* MSc by Research University of York. https://etheses.whiterose.ac.uk/8752/1/MSc%20Dissertation%20WReO.pdf

8. Murphy, T. 16 September 2015. "You call this progress?" *Do the Math.* https://dothemath.ucsd.edu/2015/09/you-call-this-progress

9. Hicks, S. 18 January 2010. "Coffee and the Enlightenment." https://www.stephenhicks.org/2010/01/18/coffee-and-the-enlightenment

10. Jansz, A. and Taylor, T. October 2011. "The Enlightenment: Psychoactive Globalisation." *Evolution of drug use.* https://evolutionofdruguse.wordpress.com/biology-driver/from-depressant-to-stimulant-the-enlightenment

11. Yudkin, J. and Lustig, R. 2012. *Pure, White and Deadly: How Sugar Is Killing Us and What We Can Do to Stop It.* Penguin

12. Hersh, J. and Voth, H. 2009. "Sweet diversity: Colonial goods and the rise of European living standards after 1492." *Economics Working Papers 1163*, Department of Economics and Business, Universitat Pompeu Fabra.

13. Hobsbawm, E.J. 1999. *Industry and Empire: From 1750 to the Present Day.* Penguin; 2Rev Ed edition.

14. Aizarani, J. 31 January 2023. "Leading oil demanding sectors in the OECD 2020." *Statista*. www.statista.com/statistics/307194/top-oil-consuming-sectors-worldwide

15. Canada Energy Regulator. 17 October 2018. *Market Snapshot: Petrochemical products in everyday life*. www.cer-rec.gc.ca/en/data-analysis/energy-markets/market-snapshots/2018/market-snapshot-petrochemical-products-in-everyday-life.html

16. Jones et al. 2009. "Total amounts of oil produced over the history of the industry." *International Journal of Oil Gas and Coal Technology*.

17. BP *Statistical Review of World Energy 2021* (70th edition)

18. Bentley, R. 29 August 2023. "What's Wrong With Rystad Energy's Global Oil Reserve Estimate?" *OilPrice*. https://oilprice.com/Energy/Crude-Oil/Whats-Wrong-With-Rystad-Energys-Global-Oil-Reserve-Estimate.html

19. See: Friedemann, A. 24 June 2020. "Global oil discovered 7.7 times less than consumption in 2019." *EnergySkeptic*. https://energyskeptic.com/2020/oil-discoveries-in-2015-lowest-since-1947-2016-likely-to-be-even-lower-bloomberg

20. Friedemann, A.J. 2016. *When Trucks Stop Running: Energy and the Future of Transportation*. Springer.

21. Berman, A. 18 January 2023. *They're not making oil like they used to: stealth peak oil?* www.artberman.com/2023/01/18/theyre-not-making-oil-like-they-used-to-stealth-peak-oil

22. Watkins, T. 5 March 2020. "Because the economy, stupid!" *Consciousness of Sheep*. https://consciousnessofsheep.co.uk/2020/03/05/because-the-economy-stupid

23. Eisenstein, C. 2011. *Sacred Economics: Money, Gift, and Society in the Age of Transition*. North Atlantic Books

24. Gill, D.J. 2022. *The Long Shadow of Default: Britain's Unpaid War Debts to the United States, 1917-2020*. Yale University Press.

25. Qualman, D. 13 June 2017. *Happy motoring: Global automobile production 1900 to 2016*. www.darrinqualman.com/global-automobile-production

26. Dixon, N.F. 1994. *On the Psychology of Military Incompetence.* Pimlico.

27. Kennedy, P. 2017. *The Rise and Fall of the Great Powers.* William Collins.

28. Byrne, R. 2008. *The Secret.* Simon & Schuster

29. Laszewski, Ronald M. 2008. Peak Debt

30. Gosden, E. 5 July 2016. "Energy chiefs call for bill levy overhaul." *Telegraph.* www.telegraph.co.uk/business/2016/07/05/energy-chiefs-call-for-bill-levy-overhaul/

31. Helm, D. 2017. *Cost of Energy Review.* Assets Publishing Service. https://assets.publishing.service.gov.uk/government/uploads/system/uploads/attachment_data/file/654902/Cost_of_Energy_Review.pdf

32. Wenar, L. 2015. *Blood Oil: Tyrants, Violence, and the Rules that Run the World.* Oxford University Press.

33. Jack, I. 19 April 2013. "North Sea oil fuelled the 80s boom, but it was, and remains, strangely invisible." *Guardian.* https://www.theguardian.com/commentisfree/2013/apr/19/north-sea-oil-80s-boom

34. Mearns, E. 5 December 2013. "Compel firms to extract North Sea oil in the nation's interest." *The Conversation.* https://theconversation.com/compel-firms-to-extract-north-sea-oil-in-the-nations-interest-21197

35. Steer, G. 2 October 2023. "Renewable energy stocks hit hard by higher interest rates." *Financial Times.* www.ft.com/content/07443afb-b935-492d-8711-8c47e4353c59

36. Watkins, T. 11 September 2023. "Blown out of the water." *Consciousness of Sheep.* https://consciousnessofsheep.co.uk/2023/09/11/blown-out-of-the-water

37. Pielke, R. 30 September 2019. "Net-Zero Carbon Dioxide Emissions By 2050 Requires A New Nuclear Power Plant Every Day." *Forbes.* www.forbes.com/sites/rogerpielke/2019/09/30/net-zero-carbon-dioxide-emissions-by-2050-requires-a-new-nuclear-power-plant-every-day

38. Cobb, K. 1 October 2023. "The clean energy economy turns out to be the metals energy economy." *Resource Insights.* http://resourceinsights.blogspot.com/2023/10/the-clean-energy-economy-turns-out-to.html

39. Michaux, S.P. 2021. *Assessment of the Extra Capacity Required of Alternative Energy Electrical Power Systems to Completely Replace Fossil Fuels.* Geological Survey of Finland.

About the Author

Tim Watkins is the author of the *Consciousness of Sheep* website and the 2015 book of the same name, which addresses the unfolding environmental, energy and resource depletion, and economic crises that threaten the collapse of industrial civilisation; and possibly the extinction of the entire human race.

He graduated from University of Wales College Cardiff with a First Class economic and social science degree in 1990.

Between 1990 and 1997 he worked as a policy researcher with the Welsh Consumer Council where he wrote and published several key policy reports including: *Quality of Life and Quality of Service* – an investigation into the provision of residential care homes for older people - and *In Deep Water* – an investigation into the many problems that followed the North Wales (Towyn) floods of February 1990.

Between 1998 and 2010, Tim Watkins worked for the charity Depression Alliance Cymru, initially as a development worker, and between 2003 and 2010 as its Director. During that time he produced several mental health publications for the charity. Between 2001 and 2010 Tim Watkins was appointed to sit on several Welsh Government advisory bodies including the Health and Wellbeing Council for Wales, the Burrows-Greenwell Review of Mental Health Services in Wales and the Expert Panel on Depression.

Since 2010, Tim Watkins has authored a range of books relating to the "three E's" - Energy, Environment and the Economy. He has also produced a range of mental health and well being self-help books and booklets, together with two books on charity.

To find out more, please visit: www.consciousnessofsheep.co.uk

You can also follow Tim Watkins on social media:

www.facebook.com/cosheep

www.youtube.com/@consciousnessofsheep

Books by Tim Watkins

The Consciousness of Sheep

The Consciousness of Sheep provides a detailed and thoroughly researched explanation of the current predicament of Western civilisation; the ways in which the crises are likely to unfold; and the progressive responses that are beginning to emerge. It is a fascinating read for anyone interested in energy, economics, the environment, and the future of the human race. The message is stark but ultimately positive – it is time for us to develop a sustainable way of life for all of humanity.

The Death Cult

Humanity faces a bottleneck of crises which threaten the collapse of industrial civilisation. Of these, most people are only aware of climate change, which most believe can be solved via electrification and a range of simple changes to our lifestyles. But climate change is just one of myriad crises, including: antibiotic resistance, biodiversity loss, chemical pollution, cyber-attacks/AI, energy shortages, famine, financial crises, governance failure, infrastructure failure, microplastic contamination, migration waves, natural disasters, nutrient run-off, ocean acidification, resource depletion, soil depletion, war, water shortages, weapons of mass destruction, to name but a few.

Any one of these crises threatens to undermine our complex industrial civilisation. But taken together, they constitute an existential threat to humanity as a whole. And yet, faced with this dire predicament, no "great leader" has come to the fore. Nor have "we the people" rallied to action. Instead, our self-identifying leaders seem impotent, while the population at large is passive. Why should this be?

Why Don't Lions Chase Mice?

In *Why Don't Lions Chase Mice*, Tim Watkins explains that without a theory of energy and with a poor and erroneous theory of money, the "experts" and politicians charged with leading us out of the gathering crises – banking and financial collapse, unemployment, under-employment and depression, energy shortages, resource depletion, environmental destruction and climate change – are leading us down a blind alley. Only when we understand the essential role of energy in the economy can we properly understand the stark choices before us.

Decline and fall: the Brexit years

On 23 June 2016 the British political landscape changed forever. Against the advice of the establishment, the British people had unexpectedly voted to leave the European Union; something that none of the political leaders had planned for. In Decline and Fall: the Brexit years, Tim Watkins sets out the long process of decline which provides the context in which the three years of political tragicomedy that followed the result should properly be seen; before presenting a compilation of three-years' of Brexit-related articles from his Consciousness of Sheep website.

The Root of all Evil: The problem of debt-based money

When the Mafia make money they use the same plates, paper and ink as the government. They include the same security features and use the same serial numbers. Even to the most trained eyes this counterfeit currency is physically indistinguishable from the real thing. This being the case, why – exactly – is this Mafia money a crime? Who are its victims? Why should we care? The answers to these questions draw us into the fraud at the heart of our contemporary financial system; a fraud so vast in its scope yet so cleverly disguised that almost all of us treat it as normal while less than one in a million ever sees it. It is the fraud of debt-based money.

The Energy Theory of Value... and its consequences

Karl Marx was 95 percent correct when he reasoned that one or more of the inputs into production must be paid far less than the value it generates in order to produce profit or "surplus value" at the end. Marx arrived at the blindingly obvious – and entirely wrong – conclusion that this input was labour. What Marx began to see toward the end of his life was that while labour could be exploited, automation meant that something else must be generating surplus value... That "something else" turns out to be Energy!

Britain's Coming Energy Crisis

We dare not talk about this... Politicians dare not discuss it for fear of causing mass panic... North Sea oil and gas production peaked in 1999. The oil bonanza is over – the oil income spent. Britain is once again an energy importer. Worse still, we are increasingly dependent upon imports from the world's trouble spots and hostile regimes – Libya, Nigeria, several Gulf States and Russia. Even worse, successive governments have failed to invest in new electricity generation; let alone a switch from petroleum-powered vehicles...

Austerity... will kill the economy

The same message has been trotted out time and again by economists and politicians from all parties: "We must pay off the debt," "We have to balance the books," "We should have fixed the roof when the sun was shining," "Only by cutting public spending can we hope to return to economic growth." What if they are wrong? What if austerity causes recession? The early cuts triggered a recession, and economic growth has been anaemic ever since. What if these are the direct consequence of a misguided policy of austerity?

On Mental Health

Defeat Depression: A Self-Help Guide

Defeat Depression is the latest self-help book from Tim Watkins. It builds upon his earlier Depression Workbook and incorporates information on the new science of willpower. This explains why so many of us fall back into habits of thought and behaviour that exacerbate depression; and what we can do to overcome them. The book offers the reader a comprehensive approach to self-help for depression that actually works. *Defeat Depression* is written in plain language, and provides the reader with 80 self-help techniques that can be easily included in a daily routine in order to begin the journey out of depression. The publication of Defeat Depression is timely, as its author, Tim Watkins explains:

> "Depression has always been with us. But since the economic downturn in 2008, more and more people have developed the

condition. Sadly, the consequence of this is that therapies like CBT (cognitive behavioural therapy) and mindfulness have become even harder to access. Far too many people are being left with little more than a packet of pills and a sicknote.

"However, many people affected by depression – myself included – have struggled to understand what helps and what hinders recovery. Drawing on both my own experience and my research among many others affected by depression, I have developed a structure that allows individuals with depression to understand the self-help process and to develop simple lifestyle changes that promote recovery."

As Watkins explains in *Defeat Depression*, self-help is neither an alternative nor a complement to conventional treatments like antidepressants and talking therapies. Rather, conventional treatments are an important part of a much broader process of self-help in which we learn to promote our own mental wellbeing and manage our own recovery from common mental illnesses like anxiety and depression.

No More Panic

Half of us will experience a panic attack at some time in our lives. For those who do, the experience can be quite literally terrifying. For many the experience is so unpleasant that they avoid similar situations in future. Some develop disabling panic disorders and agoraphobia.

At several times in his life - especially during a severe episode of mixed anxiety and depression, author Tim Watkins experienced disabling panic attacks. Then, quite by accident, he discovered a secret about panic attacks that led to recovery and to his never having a panic attack again. In this book, he sets out what he - and others - have learned about panic attacks, and how anyone can overcome them... Permanently.

Helping Hands: How to help someone else cope with mental health problems

Did you know that the worst thing people do when a family member, friend, neighbour or colleague is struggling with mental health problems, is to do nothing? Not out of spite or stigma, but ironically, because most of us are scared of saying or doing the wrong thing.

This is why I wrote *Helping hands*. *Helping Hands* helps to make you a skilled lay-helper, providing appropriate support and encouragement to the person you care about. Helping Hands will provide you with an understanding of wellbeing, and knowledge of mental illness, and will show you how you can help and support someone who has, or is at risk of developing, a mental health problem.

Helping Hands also sets out a great deal of what has been learned about self-help and self-management strategies for recovery from mental illness over the last 25 years.

Printed in Great Britain
by Amazon